Bloom's BioCritiques

Dante Alighieri
Maya Angelou
Jane Austen
The Brontë Sisters
Lord Byron
Geoffrey Chaucer
Anton Chekhov
Joseph Conrad
Stephen Crane
Charles Dickens
Emily Dickinson
William Faulkner
F. Scott Fitzgerald
Robert Frost
Ernest Hemingway
Langston Hughes
Stephen King
Arthur Miller
John Milton
Toni Morrison
Edgar Allan Poe
J. D. Salinger
William Shakespeare
John Steinbeck
Mark Twain
Alice Walker
Walt Whitman
Tennessee Williams

Bloom's BioCritiques

MARK TWAIN

Edited and with an introduction by
Harold Bloom
Sterling Professor of the Humanities
Yale University

CHELSEA HOUSE
P U B L I S H E R S
A Haights Cross Communications Company

Philadelphia

10 9 8 7 6 5 4 3 2 1

Library of Congress Cataloging-in-Publication Data

Mark Twain / edited and with an introduction by Harold Bloom.
    p. cm. -- (Bloom's biocritiques)
Includes bibliographical references and index.
Contents: Biography of Mark Twain -- Mark Twain: "The Lincoln Of Our
Language" / Tenley Williams -- Mark Twain's Civil War: humor's
reconstructive writing / Neil Schmitz -- Joyous heresy: travelling with the
innocent abroad / Henry B. Wonham -- Introduction to The Adventures of
Tom Sawyer & The Adventures of Huckleberry Finn / Stuart Hutchinson.
    ISBN 0-7910-6372-0 (0-7910-7175-8)
    1. Twain, Mark, 1835–1919--Criticism and interpretation. [1. Twain,
Mark, 1835–1910--Criticism and interpretation. 2. American literature--
History and criticism.] I. Bloom, Harold. II. Series.
    PS1338 .M27 2002
    818'.409--dc21

                                        2002152672

Chelsea House Publishers
1974 Sproul Road, Suite 400
Broomall, PA 19008-0914

http://www.chelseahouse.com

Contributing editor: Tenley Williams

Cover design by Keith Trego

Cover: Bettmann/CORBIS

Layout by EJB Publishing Services

CONTENTS

USER'S GUIDE

These volumes are designed to introduce the reader to the life and work of the world's literary masters. Each volume begins with Harold Bloom's essay "The Work in the Writer" and a volume-specific introduction also written by Professor Bloom. Following these unique introductions is an engaging biography that discusses the major life events and important literary accomplishments of the author under consideration.

Furthermore, each volume includes an original critique that not only traces the themes, symbols, and ideas apparent in the author's works, but strives to put those works into a cultural and historical perspective. In addition to the original critique is a brief selection of significant critical essays previously published on the author and his or her works followed by a concise and informative chronology of the writer's life. Finally, each volume concludes with a bibliography of the writer's works, a list of additional readings, and an index of important themes and ideas.

HAROLD BLOOM

The Work in the Writer

Literary biography found its masterpiece in James Boswell's *Life of Samuel Johnson*. Boswell, when he treated Johnson's writings, implicitly commented upon Johnson as found in his work, even as in the great critic's life. Modern instances of literary biography, such as Richard Ellmann's lives of W. B. Yeats, James Joyce, and Oscar Wilde, essentially follow in Boswell's pattern.

That the writer somehow is in the work, we need not doubt, though with William Shakespeare, writer-of-writers, we almost always need to rely upon pure surmise. The exquisite rancidities of the Problem Plays or Dark Comedies seem to express an extraordinary estrangement of Shakespeare from himself. When we read or attend *Troilus and Cressida* and *Measure for Measure*, we may be startled by particular speeches of Ulysses in the first play, or of Vincentio in the second. These speeches, of Ulysses upon hierarchy or upon time, or of Duke Vincentio upon death, are too strong either for their contexts or for the characters of their speakers. The same phenomenon occurs with Parolles, the military impostor of *All's Well That Ends Well*. Utterly disgraced, he nevertheless affirms: "Simply the thing I am/Shall make me live."

In Shakespeare, more even than in his peers, Dante and Cervantes, meaning always starts itself again through excess or overflow. The strongest of Shakespeare's creatures—Falstaff, Hamlet, Iago, Lear, Cleopatra—have an exuberance that is fiercer than their plays can contain. If Ben Jonson was at all correct in his complaint that "Shakespeare wanted art," it could have been only in a sense that he may not have intended. Where do the personalities of Falstaff or Hamlet touch a limit? What was it in Shakespeare that made the two parts of *Henry IV* and *Hamlet* into "plays unlimited"? Neither Falstaff nor Hamlet will be stopped: their wit, their beautiful, laughing speech, their intensity of being—all these are virtually infinite.

In what ways do Falstaff and Hamlet manifest the writer in the work? Evidently, we can never know, or know enough to answer with any authority. But what would happen if we reversed the question, and asked: How did the work form the writer, Shakespeare?

Of Shakespeare's inwardness, his biography tells us nothing. And yet, to an astonishing extent, Shakespeare created our inwardness. At the least, we can speculate that Shakespeare so lived his life as to conceal the depths of his nature, particularly as he rather prematurely aged. We do not have Shakespeare on Shakespeare, as any good reader of the Sonnets comes to realize: they do not constitute a key that unlocks his heart. No sequence of sonnets could be less confessional or more powerfully detached from the poet's self.

The German poet and universal genius, Goethe, affords a superb contrast to Shakespeare. Of Goethe's life, we know more than everything; I wonder sometimes if we know as much about Napoleon or Freud or any other human being who ever has lived, as we know about Goethe. Everywhere, we can find Goethe in his work, so much so that Goethe seems to crowd the writing out, just as Byron and Oscar Wilde seem to usurp their own literary accomplishments. Goethe, cunning beyond measure, nevertheless invested a rival exuberance in his greatest works that could match his personal charisma. The sublime outrageousness of the Second Part of *Faust*, or of the greater lyric and meditative poems, form a Counter-Sublime to Goethe's own daemonic intensity.

Goethe was fascinated by the daemonic in himself; we can doubt that Shakespeare had any such interests. Evidently, Shakespeare abandoned his acting career just before he composed *Measure for Measure* and *Othello*. I surmise that the egregious interventions by Vincentio and Iago displace the actor's energies into a new kind of mischief-making, a fresh opening to a subtler playwriting-within-the-play.

But what had opened Shakespeare to this new awareness? The answer is the work in the writer, *Hamlet* in Shakespeare. One can go further: it was not so much the play, *Hamlet*, as the character Hamlet, who changed Shakespeare's art forever.

Hamlet's personality is so large and varied that it rivals Goethe's own. Ironically Goethe's Faust, his Hamlet, has no personality at all, and is as colorless as Shakespeare himself seems to have chosen to be. Yet nothing could be more colorful than the Second Part of *Faust*, which is peopled by an astonishing array of monsters, grotesque devils, and classical ghosts.

A contrast between Shakespeare and Goethe demonstrates that in each—but in very different ways—we can better find the work in the person, than we can discover that banal entity, the person in the work. Goethe to many of his contemporaries, seemed to be a mortal god. Shakespeare, so far as we know, seemed an affable, rather ordinary fellow, who aged early and became somewhat withdrawn. Yet Faust, though Mephistopheles battles for his soul, is hardly worth the trouble unless you take him as an idea and not as a person. Hamlet is nearly every-idea-in-one, but he is precisely a personality and a person.

Would Hamlet be so astonishingly persuasive if his father's ghost did not haunt him? Falstaff is more alive than Prince Hal, who says that the devil haunts him in the shape of an old fat man. Three years before composing the final *Hamlet*, Shakespeare invented Falstaff, who then never ceased to haunt his creator. Falstaff and Hamlet may be said to best represent the work in the writer, because their influence upon Shakespeare was prodigious. W.H. Auden accurately observed that Falstaff possesses infinite energy: never tired, never bored, and absolutely both witty and happy until Hal's rejection destroys him. Hamlet too has infinite energy, but in him it is more curse than blessing.

Falstaff and Hamlet can be said to occupy the roles in Shakespeare's invented world that Sancho Panza and Don Quixote possess in Cervantes's. Shakespeare's plays from 1610 on (starting with *Twelfth Night*) are thus analogous to the Second Part of Cervantes's epic novel. Sancho and the Don overtly jostle Cervantes for authorship in the Second Part, even as Cervantes battles against the impostor who has pirated a continuation of his work. As a dramatist, Shakespeare manifests the work in the writer more indirectly. Falstaff's prose genius is revived in the scapegoating of Malvolio by Maria and Sir Toby Belch, while Falstaff's darker insights are developed by Feste's melancholic wit. Hamlet's intellectual resourcefulness, already deadly, becomes poisonous in Iago and in Edmund. Yet we have not crossed into the deeper abysses of the work in the writer in later Shakespeare.

No fictive character, before or since, is Falstaff's equal in self-trust. Sir John, whose delight in himself is contagious, has total confidence both in his self-awareness and in the resources of his language. Hamlet, whose self is as strong, and whose language is as copious, nevertheless distrusts both the self and language. Later Shakespeare is, as it were, much under the influence both of Falstaff and of Hamlet, but they tug him in opposite directions. Shakespeare's own copiousness of language is well-nigh incredible: a vocabulary in excess of twenty-one thousand words, almost eighteen hundred of which he coined himself. And of his word-hoard, nearly half are used only once each, as though the perfect setting for each had been found, and need not be repeated. Love for language and faith in language are Falstaffian attributes. Hamlet will darken both that love and that faith in Shakespeare, and perhaps the Sonnets can best be read as Falstaff and Hamlet counterpointing against one another.

Can we surmise how aware Shakespeare was of Falstaff and Hamlet, once they had played themselves into existence? *Henry IV, Part I* appeared in six quarto editions during Shakespeare's lifetime; *Hamlet* possibly had four. Falstaff and Hamlet were played again and again at the Globe, but Shakespeare knew also that they were being read, and he must have had contact with some of those readers. What would it have been like to discuss Falstaff or Hamlet with one of their early readers (presumably also part of their audience at the Globe), if you were the creator of such demiurges? The question would seem nonsensical to most Shakespeare scholars, but then these days they tend to be either ideologues or moldy figs. How can we recover the uncanniness of Falstaff and of Hamlet, when they now have become so familiar?

A writer's influence upon himself is an unexplored problem in criticism, but such an influence is never free from anxieties. The biocritical problem (which this series attempts to explore) can be divided into two areas, difficult to disengage fully. Accomplished works affect the author's life, and also affect her subsequent writings. It is simpler for me to surmise the effect of *Mrs. Dalloway* and *To the Lighthouse* upon Woolf's late *Between the Acts*, than it is to relate Clarissa Dalloway's suicide and Lily Briscoe's capable endurance in art to the tragic death and complex life of Virginia Woolf.

There are writers whose lives were so vivid that they seem sometimes to obscure the literary achievement: Byron, Wilde, Malraux, Hemingway. But most major Western writers do not live that exuberantly, and the greatest of all, Shakespeare, sometimes appears to have adopted the personal mask of colorlessness. And yet there are heroes of literature who struggled titanically with their own eras— Tolstoy, Milton, Victor Hugo—who nevertheless matter more for their works than their lives.

There are great figures—Emily Dickinson, Wallace Stevens, Willa Cather—who seem to have had so little of the full intensity of life when compared to the vitality of their work, that we might almost speak of the work in the work, rather than even of the work in a person. Emily Brontë might well be the extreme instance of such a visionary, surpassing William Blake in that one regard.

I conclude this general introduction to a series of literary bio-critiques by stating a tentative formula or principle for gauging the many ways in which the work influences the person and her subsequent, later work. Our influence upon ourselves is always related to the Shakespearean invention of self-overhearing, which I have written about in several other contexts. Life, as well as poetry and prose, is overheard rather than simply heard. The writer listens to herself as though she were somebody else, and the will to change begins to operate. The forces that live in us include the prior work we have done, and the dreams and waking visions that evade our dismissals.

HAROLD BLOOM

Introduction

For a country obsessed with the image of freedom, Huck Finn is an inevitable hero, since he incarnates the genius of American solitude. Richard Poirier observes that *Adventures of Huckleberry Finn* is marked by the quietness of its autobiographical narrator. Huck talks to us, the readers, but only rarely to the other figures in the book, even to his companion Jim. Loneliness is the condition of Huck's existence; he belongs neither to the adult world, nor to that world's antechamber in Tom Sawyer's gang. Truly, Huck is as isolated and eccentric a figure as "Walt Whitman," the hero of *Song of Myself*, and Mark Twain, as Poirier remarks, never found a fit context for Huck after the first sixteen chapters of *Adventures*. Partly this may mean that Huck is larger and more vital than his book, admirable as it is. But I suspect that ultimately Huck stands for what is least sociable in Mark Twain, whose discomfort with American culture was profound. Like Huck, Twain had decided to go to hell, if that was the only way to escape his neighbors and country, and if that was the only path to freedom.

Since Huck is neither a god nor a beast, he suffers intensely from his loneliness. If you define freedom as a relationship within society, then Huck is a negative image only—the hero as misfit. Classic American literature, however, does not easily permit societal definitions of freedom. Hester Prynne in *The Scarlet Letter*, Ishmael in *Moby-Dick*, Thoreau at Walden Pond, Emerson confronting the past: all provide

1

images of isolation as an inner freedom, and the exiles of Henry James have a way of reestablishing their American solitude in centers of sociability like London and Rome. Whitman proclaims the love of brothers while finding his particular metaphor for poetic creativity in Onanism, and Emily Dickinson's self-segregation is notorious. The tradition does not vary that much in the great writers of the 20th century, whose poets remain lonely: Robert Frost, Wallace Stevens, T.S. Eliot, Hart Crane, Elizabeth Bishop, John Ashbery. One thinks of the protagonists of our major novelists: Dreiser's Carrie, Cather's Ántonia, Fitgerald's Gatsby, Faulkner's Joe Christmas: these are also isolated dreamers. The American religion of self-reliance carries with it the burden that no American feels wholly free until she is truly alone.

Fitzgerald, Hemingway, and Faulkner all exalted *Adventures of Huckleberry Finn*, seeing in it their American starting point. Their tributes were rather fierce: Fitzgerald said that Huck's "eyes were the first eyes that ever looked at us objectively that were not eyes from overseas," while Hemingway placed the book first among all our books, and Faulkner's final novel, *The Reivers*, explicitly presents itself as a revision of Twain's masterpiece. What disconcerts many critics of *Huckleberry Finn*—the slippage between Huck as narrator, lying his way to a kind of freedom, and Huck as active character, ultimately manifesting a generosity of spirit beyond everyone else in the book except Jim—seems not to have bothered Twain's novelist descendants. Twain gave them a fascinating fourteen-year-old quasi-scoundrel in Huck, a trickster as resourceful as Homer's Odysseus or the biblical Jacob. Though Huck may look like an unvarying picaresque hero, he actually is a master of disguises, and he changes incessantly, while growing no older. He is very hard to characterize because he is not still long enough for us to know exactly who he is. Nor is his own sense of identity securely established: he both is and is not his dreadful father's son.

Huck's central freedom is essentially authentic: he always will be fourteen years old, because we cannot envision him, say, at forty. Lighting out for the territory will not age him; whether his morally ambiguous attitude towards society could survive maturation is therefore an inappropriate question. That may be why *Adventures of Huckleberry Finn* ends in a fashion unsatisfactory to nearly every critical reader the book has attracted. We all want Huck to be better and stronger, and even more self-reliant than he is. He has broken with the morality of slaveholding, but the break has ravaged and confused him. We cannot have a politically correct Huck, which is why the book continues to offend so many, who simply do not know enough nineteenth-century American history to see that—for his time, in his place—Huck is a miracle of self-emancipation. Yet he is not only pursued by the murderous Pap Finn; he also carries much of his father within him, as Harold Beaver has shown. *Adventures of Huckleberry Finn* has only a few rivals as the indispensable work of nineteenth-century American literature: *Moby-Dick*, *Leaves of Grass*, *The Scarlet Letter* are among them. Ahab, "Walt Whitman," Hester Prynne all inform our sense of ourselves, but it is primarily in Huck Finn that we study our nostalgias.

NORMA JEAN LUTZ

Biography of Mark Twain

AN HONORARY DEGREE FROM OXFORD

In the summer of 1907, a steamer from the United States disembarked
at a British port. When a familiar man appeared—sporting a wild mane
of white hair and dressed in a dapper white suit—the welcoming crowd
sent up a deafening cheer. Even the common stevedores working on the
docks laid aside their work and joined in the jubilant shouts and wild
applause.

The 72-year-old visitor was author, philosopher, lecturer, and
world traveler Samuel Langhorne Clemens, better known as Mark
Twain. Beloved by British citizens from all walks of life, the Missouri-
born Twain had won them over with his witty, humorous writings and
lectures, as well as his winsome personality. As a result of his many
excursions to England, the mutual affection between Twain and the
British Commonwealth only grew in intensity. The staid and proper
Brits loved him; he had an easy way of making people laugh at
themselves. Twain returned to England in 1907 to accept an award that
pleased him immensely—an honorary degree from the esteemed Oxford
University. When writing to a friend about the event, he said, "Although
I wouldn't cross an ocean again for the price of the ship that carried me,
I am glad to do it for an Oxford degree."

His original plan was to attend a few events, visit friends, accept his
award, and return home to the United States. His hosts had other ideas;

5

Mark Twain found himself amidst a whirl of social activities and appearances. Ralph Ashcroft, a gentleman who traveled with Twain as his personal secretary, could barely keep track of the many events. There were lunches, teas, receptions, and banquets to attend in addition to concerts and operas. Twain was even an honorary guest at a royal celebration, where he chatted like old friends with King Edward VII, having met His Royal Highness previously before he ascended the throne. Everyone wanted to see or talk to the world-famous author; and reporters followed him relentlessly. He used the lobby of his hotel as a sitting room for receiving guests.

Coinciding with Twain's arrival was an unrelated incident, the apparent theft of the Ascot Cup (a trophy presented to the winner of England's famous horse race). In jest, the press earmarked Twain as the culprit, which allowed for a running joke, enjoyed by all, to be perpetrated throughout his stay. Later during his visit, as he was entertained at a dinner in his honor at the Savage Club, Twain was presented with a replica of the Ascot Cup. In place of the acorn that graced the real cup was a bust of Mark Twain.

The actual presentation of the honorary degree involved a commencement parade, where the people greeted him with wild applause. Proud of his Oxford robes and mortarboard, he would later wear them for his daughter Clara's wedding.

The originally scheduled short stay stretched into more than a month before Twain returned home. He was still disconsolate by the death of his wife three years earlier, and the visit had bolstered his spirits as nothing else could. For an impoverished, uneducated boy from Hannibal, Missouri, the honorary degree was certainly the hallmark of a long and illustrious career. How Samuel Clemens achieved such fame is a remarkable rags-to-riches tale that rivals any of the stories he penned under the name of Mark Twain.

THE BAREFOOT MISSOURI BOY

Though he was raised in Missouri, Mark Twain's family originated from Kentucky; John Marshall Clemens, Twain's father, came to the state as a child in the early 1800s. His parents, like many settlers of that time, were in search of affordable land to build a homestead. A short time after their arrival, John's father, Samuel Clemens, died in an accident during a house-raising—the joint construction of a house by members of the community. John's mother soon remarried to a man who paid scant attention to the children—as a result of this, John grew up receiving little or no affection.

John left the household as soon as possible and obtained an apprenticeship in Virginia. When the apprenticeship did not work out, John again returned to Kentucky, where he studied and entered the bar as a lawyer in 1822. Perhaps due to the loss of his father at a young age, John grew up a dour, serious man who seldom laughed or joked and rarely seemed to enjoy the good moments in life.

One day, two brothers by the name of Lampton hired John Clemens to represent them in a bankruptcy case. While Clemens lost the case, he won the hand of Benjamin Lampton's red-haired daughter, Jane.

Jane Lampton, quite John's opposite, was an outgoing, vivacious girl, known for her love of dancing and her great sense of humor. While Jane's family could trace their roots back to British nobility, their financial standing was fragile at best. Jane's mother died in 1818 when Jane was barely 15, and since the Lamptons' debts were overwhelming the family, Jane entered into a hasty marriage with John Clemens. She later admitted she entered into marriage on the heels of another failed romance. While their relationship demonstrated respect and kindness, romantic love was sorely lacking between the couple.

The Clemens' moved several times during the early years of their marriage. John attempted to become a shopkeeper while his neighbors appointed him to serve as county commissioner and court clerk. In spite of his credentials as an attorney, legal work was sparse on the frontier. Thinking to make a wise investment, John purchased thousands of acres of land, which turned out to be of poor quality and would grow little more than potatoes.

John's family began to grow when a son, Orion, arrived in 1825, followed by Pamela in 1827. A sickly son who they named Pleasant Hannibal arrived in 1828, and yet another daughter, Margaret, was born in 1830. After they moved to Tennessee in search of better farmland, a fifth child, Benjamin, arrived in 1832.

As each of John's ventures met with failure, he set his sights further west. Jane's sister Martha Ann (called Patsy by family members) and her husband, John Quarles, lived in the small town of Florida, Missouri.

Jane and Patsy's father, Ben, had also moved to the town along with his second wife. The family members encouraged the Clemens to join them, which they did.

Jane was overjoyed to be back with her family once again, in spite of the fact that she had to live in a two-room cabin with a lean-to kitchen. On November 30, 1835, their first year in Missouri, she gave birth prematurely to a son. Because he was so frail, and because she had little hope that he would live, she couldn't bear to even name him. Instead, John did the honor, naming his son Samuel Langhorne Clemens— Samuel for the father John had lost, and Langhorne for the relative to whom he was apprenticed as a young man. Neither were people he particularly admired. Perhaps John, too, did not expect the child to live.

At the time of Samuel's birth, the brilliant phenomenon of Halley's Comet made its appearance in the nighttime skies. It may have been an omen, but a good one, for the Clemens family, because the frail baby continued to gain strength. Though he remained sickly for the first few years, with Jane constantly giving him terrible-tasting medicines and applying ointments, the youngest Clemens eventually began to thrive. Because of the comet, Jane never stopped thinking that her son possessed supernatural abilities.

Unlike his older siblings whose family life was often limited to their relationships with their parents, Samuel Clemens enjoyed the attention of happy, jovial, fun-loving relatives. His uncle John Quarles and his Grandfather Lampton were men who promoted joy in life and loved to tell a good story. Samuel basked in the attention of all the family members, and by imitating his mother's slow way of speaking, he found he could make people laugh. At an early age, Samuel Clemens learned the joys of being center stage.

His serious father, meanwhile, became a judge in the county court. Extremely civic minded, John attempted to have Florida chosen as the county seat. Though he fought hard, the town was rejected for not meeting the standards of county officials. In yet another venture, he took steps to raise money to have the Salt River dredged and straightened, but this project was also doomed to failure.

Samuel Clemens' earliest memories included slaves and a slave culture. Even though Clemens counted many slaves among his acquaintances, he was taught early in life that they were different from white people and that they lacked certain fundamental rights. He was especially close to Uncle Dan, a slave belonging to the Quarleses, who served as his father figure. While young Clemens talked with the slaves, and even played with the slave children, he never ate a meal with them. Segregation was clear and absolute in Missouri in the 1830s.

For many years, a slave by the name of Jenny worked as nursemaid to the Clemens children. At the tender age of six, Samuel Clemens watched as his father tied Jenny's hands with a leather bridle and mercilessly beat the woman. Another slave named Lewis suffered beatings by John simply because he was awkward and clumsy. Such images were deeply imbedded in Clemens' mind as a child and caused no end of confusion. "... I was not aware that there was anything wrong about it. No one arraigned it in my hearing; the local papers said nothing against it; the local pulpit taught us that God approved it, that it was a holy thing, and that the doubter need only look to the Bible"....

Nationwide economic problems, along with the rapid growth of the West, caused the little river town of Florida to suffer greatly. In desperation, Sam's father began to look for greener pastures. In the summer of 1838, Samuel Clemens had to make way for the arrival of a younger brother named Henry. A few months after Henry's birth, John left the family to go check on his lands in Tennessee. At the same time, Clemens' aunt and uncle Quarles moved to a farm outside of town. As his young world fell apart, Clemens began sleepwalking each night, usually in the direction of his mother's bed.

As he was sleepwalking one night in August 1839, young Clemens walked to the bed of his sister, Margaret, and touched her bedclothes. When Margaret became ill and died a few days later, Clemens' mother looked upon his action as a premonition of her death. The confused child, understanding nothing about premonitions, felt he had *caused* his sister's death. It was the beginning of a confusion and guilt that would stay with him for a lifetime.

Soon after Margaret's death the family once again became uprooted, as John moved them to the Mississippi River town of Hannibal, Missouri. Samuel Clemens suffered many losses in the move, not the least of which was the love and admiration of his extended family. In his future writings, the town of Florida would forever be blended in with his memories of Hannibal.

Hannibal, a much larger town than Florida, boasted a 60-foot-wide Main Street, more than 1,000 inhabitants, and a constant flow of river traffic, with steamboats stopping there three times a week. The town offered amazing possibilities for wealth and prosperity, but most of it stayed just out of the reach of the Clemens family. Paying off creditors became a constant worry for John Clemens.

In spite of his indebtedness, John enjoyed the respect of the townspeople. As an acting judge, he presided over a trial involving three abolitionists who had taken slaves north to freedom. Judge Clemens gave them a stiff sentence of 12 years in the penitentiary, which drew cheers from his friends and supporters in Hannibal. Thus Samuel Clemens saw his father's moment of glory result from his support of slavery.

In the spring of 1842, tragedy again struck the Clemens household when nine-year-old Ben died. The shock for the family, still reeling from the loss of Margaret, was almost too much to bear.

To satisfy her need for more family support, Samuel Clemens' mother took the youngest of her children to spend summers at the Quarles farm. Orion, now a teenager, remained in Hannibal to help his father with the family store. The farm gave Samuel the freedom from his somber father that he desperately craved.

Clemens began to learn techniques of storytelling from the dozen or so slaves at the farm. One particularly scary ghost story, "The Golden Arm," told by Uncle Dan, would one day be narrated by Clemens to audiences around the world. And Uncle Dan, a tender, loving and patient man, would become the model for the slave named Jim in the story of Huckleberry Finn.

While there were no public schools in Hannibal, Clemens' parents paid for him to attend Mrs. Horr's dame school, where his first teacher was Mary Ann Newcomb, a family friend from Florida, Missouri. Clemens' promotion to the fourth grade brought him into the classroom of William Cross, where he was taught Latin and French.

Clemens never liked school much and preferred to skip it as often as possible. In spite of the fact that he was perfectly capable of learning, he rebelled by intentionally underachieving. On the other hand, his younger brother Henry was always well behaved, and routinely received good marks in school. It seemed the better Henry performed in school, the more Samuel's behavior and performance deteriorated.

Judge Clemens built his family a nice home on Hill Street, and it would be their first taste of prosperity. Across the street lived Laura

Hawkins, a little blonde girl who was the object of young Clemens' affections. Laura would one day serve as the model for Becky Thatcher in his book *The Adventures of Tom Sawyer.* Just up the hill lived the town drunk, along with his wife and many children. One of the children in this family, Tom Blankenship, became a close friend of Clemens. He would later use Tom Blankenship as the pattern for the character of Huckleberry Finn. While Clemens' parents disdained this friendship, they had little control over him, as he made a habit of slipping out of the house after dark.

Joining with Clemens and Tom were John Briggs, Will Bowen, John Garth, and John Robards—along with a few younger boys—all of whom formed an unruly gang looking for trouble, which they usually found with ease. The boys made rafts and floated to Glassock's Island, in the middle of the Mississippi River. They swam, fished, hunted turtle eggs, raided orchards, played games and made outrageous dares to one another. As the biggest daredevil of all, Clemens often served as the gang leader.

McDowell's cave offered some of the most fascinating exploring of all for the boys. The cave, tucked under the promontory of Lover's Leap, led to a vast maze of crooked passageways. Outlaws were said to have used the cave as a convenient hideout. One of the town drunks known as Injun Joe became lost in McDowell's cave for days. When at last he made his way out, Injun Joe said he'd survived by eating bats. Clemens and his gang played it safe by letting out kite string behind them when they explored the passageways. The cave, too, would play a role in his future books.

Tom Blankenship's older brother, Ben, discovered an escaped slave on the Illinois side of the river. Even though Ben was poor, he opted to forego the reward money he would have received by turning in the slave. Instead, he took food to the man and protected him. Eventually, however, bounty hunters found the runaway slave and chased him into the swamps, where he died. A few days later, while Clemens and his friends were fishing, they came upon the decomposed body of the slave—a terrifying experience he never forgot.

During Clemens' youth, Hannibal came into its own as a thriving community. Strategically located between St. Louis and Keokuk, Iowa, the town prospered from river trade. Whereas the steamboats once stopped three times a week, soon there were boats stopping three times a day. Fine brick buildings lined Market Street, and outlying neighborhoods featured attractive homes made of stone, brick, and clapboard—gone were the dusty streets and log cabins. People were making a fortune in the riverboat trade—everyone, it seemed, but John Clemens.

By 1847, John faced bankruptcy and the family was forced to give up their Hill Street home. A friend of his by the name of Dr. Grant allowed the family to live above his pharmacy. It became Jane's job to cook for both families, and the sudden drop in social status distressed and embarrassed her. Earlier, they'd been forced to sell the slave named Jenny; young Clemens and his siblings missed her a great deal.

In order to bolster family finances, John ran for the position of county court clerk. If elected, he would earn at least a small paycheck. Meanwhile, he continued to try selling the land in Tennessee but was unsuccessful. After traveling to another town to serve as attorney in a court case, John was caught in a sleet storm on his way home. Pneumonia ensued and caused him to be bedridden. After that, he slowly weakened.

Orion was called home from St. Louis, where he had been working, and Pamela came home from Florida. In the presence of his family, John encouraged them to hold onto the Tennessee land, which he felt would eventually be worth a fortune. Strangely, of all the family members, he called 19-year-old Pamela to his bed and gave her a final kiss before he died. The date was March 24, 1847; John Clemens was 48 years old.

Samuel Clemens felt guilty over his father's death, both for being disobedient and for resenting his father's authority. The shock of loss brought on his habit of sleepwalking once again. One night as he walked about, still asleep and wrapped in a bed sheet, his movement awakened his mother, frightening her in the process. Jane never forgot the experience.

Samuel Clemens was only eleven years old when his father died. For all practical purposes his childhood had come to an end.

THE PRINTER'S APPRENTICE

For a time after his father's death, Clemens rebelled even more fiercely than before. With Orion in St. Louis, Pamela away teaching music, and

Jane preoccupied with the family's finances, Clemens received little or no supervision.

One day, climbing high atop Holliday Hill, which rose approximately 300 feet above the Mississippi, Clemens and his gang worked to loosen a boulder perched there. The boys successfully dislodged the huge stone, which weighed about 300 pounds, as Clemens supervised. The boulder soon became too much to handle—it rolled down the hill toward a cooper's shop, bouncing over the road and over the head of a shocked black man driving a horse-drawn cart. With one last bounce the boulder landed on top of the cooper's shop, and completely demolished it. Thankfully, no one was inside.

Another time, Clemens and his friend Tom Nash decided to skate on the river as it was beginning to thaw. As the ice began to crack and break apart beneath them, they made a desperate attempt for the shore. Clemens made it, but Tom fell into the frigid waters. After being rescued, Tom contracted scarlet fever and lost his hearing.

For the first two years after his father's death, Clemens continued to attend school, but he also performed odd jobs such as delivering newspapers and helping out at various stores. Eventually he became apprenticed to Joseph Ament at the *Missouri Courier*, one of Hannibal's newspapers. The situation was arranged by Orion, who worked in a print shop in St. Louis, thus being familiar with the business.

An apprentice earned no wages; rather, he was trained with the hope of someday becoming skilled enough to earn a living in that field. Clemens' pay amounted to his room and board and whatever clothing his employer chose to supply. In this case, Ament barely provided his workers with enough to eat, and the clothes Clemens received were Ament's castoffs. Nevertheless, Clemens worked hard at his job and proved to be much more reliable than he had been as a school student. His first tasks were menial chores such as scrubbing floors, but soon he was setting type and reading proof, winning the respect of his employer.

During this time, the California gold rush fever of 1849 burned like a wildfire across the country. Clemens watched as many of his old friends and their families packed up to head out West to find their fortunes. The environment of Hannibal changed as more strangers arrived, spoiling the close-knit familiarity Clemens had known as a little boy.

This sobering time was coupled with another event that Clemens would later say changed his life. By his own admission, he'd never taken school seriously and rarely if ever applied himself to his studies. However, one day he chanced to find a loose page from a book blowing in the street. He picked it up and read it; it was about Joan of Arc. The description of the suffering she experienced touched Clemens deeply. He'd never realized the power of the written word until that moment. Suddenly he had a hunger to read and to learn, and he focused on reading history.

In January 1851, Clemens left Ament and began working for his brother Orion, who had returned to Hannibal to publish the *Hannibal Western Union*. Although Orion promised wages of $3.50 a week, he was never able to pay a cent. Samuel didn't mind because he began to write for the paper, something he enjoyed immensely.

Shortly thereafter, his sister Pamela married William Moffett, a man the family had known for years. William turned out to be a wise businessman and moved to St. Louis to set up his trade as a wholesaler.

Orion, on the other hand, was no better at business decisions than his father before him. His plan for making a profit with his paper, the name of which he changed to the *Journal*, was to reduce advertising and subscription costs. Most of his customers who did pay offered vegetables and cordwood instead of cash, making the shop look more like a store than a newspaper office.

Even though Clemens had a desire to write, Orion usually discouraged his efforts. Clemens loved humor and satire, while Orion felt the paper should be serious. Partly to spite his brother, he submitted a story to *The Carpet-Bag* magazine and was thrilled to have it accepted. The story, "The Dandy Frightening the Squatter" bore the initials "S.L.C." and appeared in the May 1, 1852 issue. Of course, 16-year-old Samuel Clemens relished showing it to his older brother.

One time when Orion had to be out of town, he left his younger brother in charge of the paper. Taking full advantage of the absence of his overbearing brother, Clemens wrote spoofs and humorous satire that would later be characteristic of his alter ego, Mark Twain. He even lampooned two prominent citizens, which caused more of a disturbance in town then Clemens thought possible. Orion's arrival back home, however, meant an end to Clemens' freedom of expression in the paper.

When *The Journal* progressed from a weekly to a daily paper, Clemens' workload increased. His younger brother Henry, who now worked by his side, could not set type well and Clemens fussed and fumed, staying up most nights to correct his mistakes. In all areas of his life, Samuel Clemens felt frustrated and trapped. He wanted the freedom to explore the world.

Clemens told his mother he wanted to go to St. Louis and become a journeyman compositor. There he could live with Pamela and her family. What he didn't tell his mother was that he had no intentions of staying in St. Louis. Knowing she could not hold her son back, Jane let him go, but made him repeat after her, "I do solemnly swear that I will not throw a card or drink a drop of liquor while I am gone."

Clemens worked at setting type for the *St. Louis Evening News* just long enough to earn enough money to go to New York. Without telling his mother, he boarded a ship and arrived in New York five days later. Back home, Orion waited expectantly for his brother's return, since it proved nearly impossible to print the paper without his help. Days stretched into weeks, and Samuel Clemens did not come home.

In New York, Clemens obtained a job at John A. Gray & Greene, a printing shop where books, magazines and journals were typeset. His wages barely covered the rent at his boarding house on Duane Street. Accustomed to being surrounded by friends and family, Clemens suffered from acute homesickness, but could not admit it. Letters from home were scarce and he chafed at their lack of communication.

No longer able to handle the workload at the paper, Orion sold it and moved to Muscatine, Iowa. Being an avowed abolitionist, Orion wanted to live on free soil where he could live according to his principles. Missouri had become too volatile for his tastes.

Clemens remained in New York only eight weeks. He moved to Philadelphia, where he did night work as a typesetter at the *Philadelphia Inquirer*. While in Philadelphia, Clemens at last received a letter from Orion explaining the family's whereabouts. Orion had taken charge of the *Muscatine Journal*, with Henry as his assistant. Soon Clemens was writing letters home describing the sights, and Orion subsequently printed them in his paper. To satisfy his brother's desire for variety in the writing, Clemens visited Washington, D.C. At this young age, Samuel Clemens showed an amazing ability to create vivid scenes that could be easily envisioned by the reader:

> The public buildings of Washington are all fine specimens of architecture, and would add greatly to the embellishment of

such a city as New York—but here they are sadly out of place
looking like so many palaces in a Hottentot village.... The
[other] buildings, almost invariably, are very poor—two and
three story brick houses, and strewed about in clusters; you
seldom see a compact square off Pennsylvania Avenue. They
look as though they might have been emptied out of a sack
by some Brobdignagian gentleman, and when falling, been
scattered abroad by the winds.

Continuing his wanderings, Clemens returned to Philadelphia and
again to New York. A fire at Gray's, however, had put a number of
typesetters out of work. Unable to find a job, he reluctantly decided it
was time to go home—but he didn't really have a home. In addition, he
felt shame that he'd been unable to send any money to his mother. In
spite of all his negative emotions, he caught a train for Muscatine in the
spring of 1854, stopping briefly in St. Louis to see Pamela.

Not much larger than Hannibal, Clemens found Muscatine to be
a boring place. He stayed with his mother and brothers, once again
working with Orion on his newspaper, and again with no wages. In the
summer, Orion married Mary Eleanor Stotts, known as Mollie, and he
moved out to create a home of his own. Just after the wedding, Clemens
felt he could bear Orion no longer, and moved back to St. Louis. Jane
quickly followed and took up residence with Pamela and Will.

While living in St. Louis, Clemens enjoyed lectures and the
theater while broadening his scope of reading to include such notables
as Charles Dickens and Sir Walter Scott. It was during this time that he
began to entertain the idea of fulfilling a childhood dream of working on
the river.

Within the year, Mollie insisted upon moving back to her
hometown of Keokuk, which lay halfway between Hannibal and
Muscatine. In Keokuk, Orion took over the Ben Franklin Job Printing
Office. As always, Orion chose to lower prices so much he was prevented
from becoming a success at the business.

In the heat of the St. Louis summer, Clemens traveled to Keokuk,
which he found a much more pleasant place than Muscatine. Mollie's
large circle of friends in Keokuk allowed him more social contacts. One
girl in particular won his attentions—Annie Taylor, whose father,
Hawkins Taylor, was a former steamboat captain.

In September 1855, Mollie gave birth to a daughter they named Jennie. Henry, now old enough to become a good friend of Clemens', also worked for Orion in the print shop. After hours, the shop became a gathering place for single male friends who sat up and talked into the wee hours of the morning. With Orion distracted by family duties and Jane in St. Louis, Clemens found a peaceful existence. His popularity gave a boost to his self-confidence, as did his first opportunity to speak in pubic.

Orion organized a banquet for the printers of Keokuk on January 7, 1856, and Clemens was requested to speak. His speech was "replete with wit and humor, being interrupted by long and continuous bursts of applause." It was an exhilarating experience for a 20-year-old.

There were, however, still problems between Clemens and Orion. Because Orion was unable to pay wages he offered Samuel partnership in the business. On the surface it appeared to be a promising offer; they divided the work between them, but whenever Clemens had a job to finish, Orion claimed the presses for printing the newspaper, leaving his brother unable to meet promised deadlines. Additionally, Orion continually reduced whatever prices Clemens agreed to for various printing jobs. Thinking he was encouraging repeat business, Orion succeeded only in operating at a loss.

Clemens' forays into love and romance were equally frustrating. While he expressed affection for Annie Taylor in his letters, he seemed confused as to how to develop a close relationship with a girl. Becoming restless once again, he talked of leaving Keokuk, and leaving the United States altogether. Having heard wild stories about millions to be made from the bounty of the Amazon, he made plans to go to South America—but first he needed money.

Leaving Keokuk, Clemens moved back to St. Louis. Before leaving, however, he arranged with the editor of the *Keokuk Post* to send back sketches of St. Louis, for which he was to receive $5 apiece. The tone of the sketches was that of an awed country bumpkin in the big city. These humorous letters, written in a fictive narrative, were signed with his pseudonym, "Thomas Jefferson Snodgrass." The readers loved his style. Describing a theater, Snodgrass wrote:

> Gals! Bless your soul, there was gals of every age and sex, from three months up to a hundred years, and every

cherubim of 'em had a fan and an opery glass and a—
tongue—probably two or three of the latter weepon, from
the racket they made. No use trying to estimate the oceans of
men and moustaches—the place looked like a shoe brush
shop.

In order to earn higher wages, Clemens traveled to Cincinnati,
which was known then as the printing center of the West. Working at T.
Wrightson and Company, he helped set the *James's River Guide*, from
which he learned a great deal more about the Ohio and the Mississippi
Rivers. For a time he continued to send sketches to the Keokuk paper,
but eventually his long work hours and other distractions slowed his
writing to a standstill.

The winter Clemens spent in Cincinnati was particularly brutal,
with the frozen Ohio River preventing delivery of coal needed for
heating. From November to February, Clemens had suffered from the
cold. On February 15, 1857, he gladly boarded the riverboat *Paul Jones*,
piloted by Captain Horace Bixby—which was headed for New Orleans
and, beyond that, the Amazon.

PILOT ON THE MISSISSIPPI

Throughout the voyage from Cincinnati to New Orleans, Clemens
spent a good deal of time hanging around Captain Bixby and watching
with interest how the old steamboat operated. Upon his arrival in New
Orleans, Clemens made two incredible discoveries. First, no one he
encountered knew anything about a ship, or any ships for that matter,
leaving for South America. And secondly, if there had been a ship
leaving, he would not have had sufficient funds to purchase a ticket.

Clemens would later write about the incident:

It had not occurred to me to inquire about these particulars
before leaving Cincinnati, so there I was. I couldn't get to the
Amazon. I had no friends in New Orleans and no money to
speak of. I went to Horace Bixby and asked him to make a
pilot out of me. He said he would do it for five hundred
dollars, one hundred dollars cash in advance.

Actually, Clemens spent many days attempting to convince Bixby to take him on as a student. The old veteran had no love for inexperienced pilots. But there must have been something about Clemens that swayed the captain, for in the end, he accepted the challenge of serving as his mentor and guide.

Of course Clemens did not have anywhere near the amount of money Bixby charged. Unsure of what to do, he asked the captain if he would accept $100 as a down payment and allow him to work off the other $400. Bixby agreed.

Knowing he would have to borrow $100, Clemens returned to St. Louis and approached a wealthy cousin by the name of James Clemens, who refused to loan him the money. At the Moffett household—which now consisted of two children, Annie and Sammy—the entire family bubbled with excitement at the prospect of Clemens becoming a river pilot. In a quiet moment, his brother-in-law, Will Moffett, took him aside and offered to loan the money. Clemens wasted no time in contacting Bixby, and the lessons began in earnest.

Steamboats on the Mississippi River did not dock in port at night. Pilots manned the wheel on four-hour shifts, running the boats through the night. Having his sleep disrupted night after night wore on Clemens very quickly. But that was by no means the worst part of his new position. Learning a thousand or more miles of unpredictable, changeable river proved to be close to impossible. Had he known just how difficult it was, Clemens was sure he'd never have wanted to become a pilot in the first place.

As they traveled, Captain Bixby called out the names of landmarks along the way. Clemens, thinking he was receiving too much needless information, paid scant attention. Later, however, Bixby asked such questions as, "What is the shape of Walnut Bend?" and Clemens did not know the answer. Later he wrote, "He might as well have asked me my grandmother's opinion of protoplasm." Admitting to the captain that he did not know, the apt teacher flew into a rage. The captain then explained to Clemens that not only would he have to know the shape of the river, but he must also know it in the dark of night, on a starlit night, in the fog, in the mist, and when there was a full moon. Each element, Bixby explained, changed a person's perception of the shapes of the river.

In addition, a pilot must know the positions of sandbars, snags, wreckages from other boats, and sawyers (partially submerged logs).

Bixby then reminded Clemens that when traveling upstream, appearances differed from looking at them going downstream. "It was plain that I had got to learn the shape of the river in all the different ways that could be thought of—upside down, wrong end first, inside out, fore-and-aft, and 'thort-ships,'—and then know what to do on gray nights when it hadn't any shape at all," Clemens said.

Bixby then told him the importance of the calls of the leadsmen and that each call in every place must be noted and remembered. In shallow water the leadsmen went ahead of the boat in a rowboat. Dropping heavy ropes into the water, they measured the depth and called back to the captain: "Mark three; quarter less three ... half twain, quarter twain, mark twain." The call, "Mark twain," denoted a depth safe enough for the boat to navigate.

"My boy," Bixby said, "you've got to remember it. You've got to remember the exact spot and the exact marks the boat lay in when we had the shoalest water, in every one of the 500 shoal places between St. Louis and New Orleans; and you mustn't get the shoal soundings and marks of one trip mixed up with the shoal soundings and marks of another, either, for they're not often twice alike. You must keep them separate."

Clemens became convinced such knowledge lay totally beyond his grasp and told Bixby so. "I want to retire from this business. I want a slush-bucket and a brush; I'm only fit for a roustabout. I haven't got brains enough to be a pilot; and if I had I wouldn't have strength enough to carry them around, unless I went on crutches."

"Now drop that!" Bixby retorted. "When I say I'll learn a man the river I mean it. And you can depend on it. I'll learn him or kill him."

With time, Clemens did learn. He purchased a notebook and made meticulous notes of everything he was told. After a year, he was considered a fine steersman, but he was still an apprentice with no wages. Whenever he had a day or two of idle time in New Orleans, Clemens guarded cargo on the docks during the night hours, earning $3 a night. The few dollars went to purchase sorely needed articles of clothing. The experience, however, proved much more profitable.

It was a desolate experience watching there in the dark among those piles of freight; not a sound, not a living creature astir. But it was not a profitless one; I used to have inspirations as I sat there alone those nights. I used to imagine all sorts of situations and possibilities. Those things got into my books by and by and furnished me with many a chapter. I can trace the effect of those nights through most of my books one way and another.

Clemens was much too busy during this time to have even a moment to write professionally. He received word that Orion had given up the Ben Franklin Printing Office and had returned to the family's roots in Jamestown, Tennessee. Orion hoped to sell the family land and use the money to study to become a lawyer. Henry, meanwhile, lived in St. Louis, where he appeared to be without direction in his life. Because Clemens was now a steersman on the lavish steamboat, the *Pennsylvania*, he found Henry a job as a clerk on the same boat.

Of the two pilots on the *Pennsylvania*, one was refined and polite; the other, William Brown, a mean-spirited and foul-mouthed man, caused Clemens no end of consternation. Finding fault with everything Clemens did, Brown made life miserable for him. For weeks, Clemens lay awake nights imagining new and innovative ways to kill William Brown. "... not in old, stale, commonplace ways, but in new and picturesque ones—ways that were sometimes surprising for freshness of design and ghastly for situation and environment."

As springtime arrived on the river, Clemens' mind turned to romance. While docked in New Orleans, the *Pennsylvania* anchored beside the *John J. Roe*. When Clemens boarded the old boat to greet his friends, he chanced to meet a lovely 14-year-old girl named Laura Wright. Laura, on vacation from her home in Missouri, where her father served as a judge, was visiting a cousin who worked on the *John J. Roe*. Clemens fell deeply in love with Laura. By the time the *Pennsylvania* backed out of the levee, the two had become inseparable. Then a disaster changed Clemens' life.

An incident in which Captain Brown unjustly accused Clemens' brother Henry of wrongdoing fueled Clemens' anger to the boiling point. He left the ship and joined the Memphis-bound *A.T. Lacy*, while Henry stayed on board the *Pennsylvania*. Only a few days later, Clemens received word that the boilers on the *Pennsylvania* had blown up near Memphis and many were killed and injured. William Brown was killed instantly.

Henry, Clemens learned, had been badly scalded and exposed to the elements for several hours before being rescued. He rushed to the makeshift hospital in Memphis and remained by Henry's bedside, nursing him until his brother died the morning of June 21, 1858. Clemens never stopped blaming himself for Henry's death.

Strangely, days earlier Clemens had experienced a vivid dream in which he saw Henry lying in a metal coffin, dressed in a suit of his own clothes with a bouquet of white roses spread out on his chest with one red rose in the center. He told the dream to his mother and his sister, who of course made light of such a worry. But after Henry died, he was indeed placed in a metal coffin, in a suit of Clemens' clothes. Some of the ladies of Memphis who had taken special interest in Henry and his brother provided the flowers—a bouquet of white roses with one red rose in the center.

Clemens' despair knew no bounds. Both friends and family members feared he might be suicidal. It was his old friends from Hannibal, the Bowens, who persuaded Clemens to go back on the river. All three Bowen boys were now river pilots. Sam Bowen got Clemens a position as steersman for the *John H. Dickey*, which made only short runs from St. Louis to Memphis. In that way, Clemens could continue his work and still remain near his family. This hastened his recovery from the incessant grief.

On April 9, 1859, Clemens' dream came true as he received his riverboat pilot license. He now moved into the elite group of pilots who enjoyed high wages and incomparable prestige. Clemens played his part to the hilt, dressing in the newest fashions, dining at the most expensive restaurants, dancing the most modern steps, and hobnobbing with the upper crust of society in river towns where his boats docked.

River pilots reigned supreme in their own separate universe, answering to no one. "Kings are but the hampered servants of parliament and people," Clemens later wrote,

> parliaments sit in chains forged by their constituency; ... but in the day I write of, the Mississippi pilot had *none*. The captain could stand upon the hurricane-deck, in the pomp of a very brief authority, and give him five or six orders while the vessel backed into the stream, and then that skipper's reign was over. The moment that boat was under way in the

river, she was under the sole and unquestioned control of the pilot.

For two years, Clemens piloted steamboats on the Mississippi River almost continuously. His record as a safe and capable pilot remained virtually spotless. He was involved in only two harbor crashes for which his captains took the blame, and he ran aground only once. These were some of the happiest times in Clemens' life. In his mind he would spend his entire life as a riverboat pilot. But circumstances beyond his control altered his plans. While the nation marched ever closer to civil war, the world Clemens knew and loved on the Mississippi River was destined to disappear forever.

Many of Clemens' friends and cohorts felt adamantly pro or con about the issues of slavery and states' rights. Clemens, at age 25, did not feel strongly either way, so he decided to remain quiet. Therefore, neither his notebooks nor his letters mention anything about the turmoil surrounding him. While Orion campaigned for the election of Abraham Lincoln as president, Clemens voted for John Bell of Tennessee, a minor-party candidate with no chance of winning.

In an attempt to take his mind off his country's problems, Clemens traveled to Warsaw, Missouri to visit Laura Wright. But their relationship, for some reason, disintegrated at this point. Pursuing another girl from Keokuk named Myra Robbins, he became discouraged after her father refused Clemens permission to court his daughter. Mr. Robbins, it seemed, did not approve of river men.

Early in 1861, Orion received word that President Lincoln had named him as secretary to the new territory of Nevada. Orion quickly moved Mollie and their daughter home to Keokuk, where he began to make plans for his trip out West. Somehow he would have to raise his own money to fund the trip.

Back in Clemens' hometown of Hannibal, he found the town patrolled by a Home Guard loyal to the Union. Some of his friends tried to persuade Clemens to join with them in resisting the Union oppression, but he still refused to commit.

In April, Confederate troops fired on Fort Sumter, launching the country into full-scale war. By May 1, Clemens was back in New Orleans. His captain, David DeHaven, a man loyal to the South, encouraged him to stay with the boat. Such an act would signify

Clemens' choice to serve with the Confederacy. Wanting to cling to his neutrality as long as possible, he boarded the *Nebraska* as a passenger and headed back north.

Already the Union forces had closed the river at Cairo, Illinois, shutting off the St. Louis trade, and Union troops were on hand to search the *Nebraska*. Just outside of St. Louis, Union soldiers opened fire on the boat, shattering the glass in the pilothouse where Clemens happened to be standing at the moment. At least one decision had been made for him—the *Nebraska* became the last boat allowed north.

Out West

For a time Clemens stayed in St. Louis, but hearing rumors that river pilots were being pressed into service for the Union, he left there and returned to Hannibal. His boyhood friends from Hannibal had organized a secessionist regiment and, not knowing what else to do, Clemens joined the regiment with them.

The ragtag regiment drilled secretly outside of town. Area residents contributed to the group by providing horses and mules for their use. Clemens was given a mule to ride; it was named Paint Brush for the way its tail was trimmed. Never a horseman, Clemens was not particularly enthused with this development.

The regiment's plan was to begin traveling south to join up with other Confederate troops. Supposedly, Clemens was considered second-in-command as the second lieutenant, but since no member of the group obeyed anyone's orders, it didn't matter much. When the weather turned rainy the men were cold, wet, hungry, and miserable. It was quite a change for Clemens from the luxuries he'd been accustomed to on board the plush riverboats.

Sympathetic farmers warned the regiment that Union troops who'd learned of their existence were in full pursuit with plans to hang them. The Rangers, as they called themselves, took refuge in a barn. When one of the men, a careless smoker, set the hay on fire, Clemens leapt out of the barn loft and received a nasty sprain to his ankle, which disabled him for a number of weeks. At that point, he was done with soldiering. "I had got part of it learned," he said. "I knew more about retreating than the man that invented retreating."

When he was able, Clemens left Missouri and headed for Orion's house in Keokuk, Iowa. Upon his arrival, Clemens offered to fund Orion's trip West if he could come along. Orion agreed, appointing him secretary to the Secretary. It was a job that promised no salary, but thus far no job Clemens ever held with Orion had ever paid a penny. Mollie and Jennie were left behind with plans for Orion to send for them once he'd settled in and found suitable residence.

The brothers left Iowa on July 26, 1861. The journey by stagecoach took them into a world far from the war and far from Samuel's identity as a dignified steamboat captain. Forced to travel light, they packed only the most basic articles of clothing, leaving fancy attire behind. They shared the coach with heavy bags of mail, which they resorted to using as makeshift mattresses.

As the pilot of a riverboat, Clemens was well acquainted with danger and threats to safety. However, out West lurked dangers of a much different sort—wildly unpredictable weather, threats of Indian attacks, and ruthless, fearless outlaws.

The bumping, jolting stagecoach traveled the distance of 100 miles a day, stopping only briefly to change horses and drivers and allowing passengers to eat. Along the way Clemens somehow felt unfettered and free. He described this experience as an

> exhilarating sense of emancipation from all sorts of cares and responsibilities, that almost made us feel that the years we had spent in the close, hot city, toiling and slaving, had been wasted and thrown away. We were spinning along through Kansas, and in the course of an hour and a half we were fairly abroad on the Great Plains.

After their arrival in Carson City, the territorial capital of Nevada, Clemens spent time studying the economics of the area, specifically mining. Mining fever hit Nevada in 1859. Serving as an assistant to Orion was not time consuming, which came as no surprise to Clemens, and it left him with time on his hands.

Thinking it would be prudent to stake a timber claim in order to sell wood to miners, he and a new friend headed to Lake Tahoe to locate a claim. Unfamiliar with camping and campfires, Clemens was unable to control an untended fire. The fire not only destroyed their claim but also discouraged him in the process. He would have to find something better suited to his abilities.

Originally Clemens had planned to stay out West for three months, thinking the war would be over and he could return to being a pilot. However, after three months, the war had only become more fierce and widespread, and Clemens had begun to enjoy the Wild West. He took to wearing a slouch hat, blue woolen shirts, pants stuffed into the tops of his boots, a full beard, and a revolver strapped to his belt. Always with an ear for language, Clemens quickly picked up on the slang and the stories of the mining towns. All the refinement he'd gained as a pilot fell away as he turned to drinking and staying up all night playing poker.

By the summer of 1862, Clemens found himself more deeply involved with the demands of mining and hating it more every day. At one point—the closest Clemens ever came to hard physical labor—he spent long hours shoveling silver-bearing ore into the pulverizing machinery. His speculations failed to make him wealthy, but they succeeded in sinking him deeply into debt.

Occasionally, Clemens continued to send his pieces out to various newspapers, one of which was the *Territorial Enterprise* in Virginia City. At a time when he detested mining but couldn't seem to part from it, he received an offer from the *Enterprise* to become a full-time reporter. Clemens' choice to take the position would change the course of his life.

While Carson City held claim to being the capital of the territory, Virginia City boasted the true silver mines and thus the higher population of the two. When Clemens arrived he found Virginia City swarming with people. Quartz wagons, freight teams, buggies, and buckboards vied for positions on the traffic-clogged main street. People waited for as long as a half hour just to cross the street.

Optimism was thriving in Virginia City; one could almost taste the excitement in the air. The growing metropolis had fire companies, brass bands, banks, hotels, theaters, shops, saloons, and no shortage of gambling. Law and order, however, was mostly lacking, with murders, robberies and fistfights considered common occurrences.

The *Territorial Enterprise*, the paper with which Clemens signed on, had become one of the finer papers in the West. Joseph T. Goodman and Dan DeQuille (pen name for William Wright) co-founded the paper after moving from San Francisco, where the two had edited a literary magazine together. The *Enterprise* straightforwardly reported the facts when writing about mining and related affairs. When it came to local news, however, a little—or a lot—of fabrication didn't seem to matter. It was a perfect setting for Samuel Clemens.

The paper, with its huge list of paying subscribers, could pay wages that Clemens sorely needed. Most of the young men on staff were near to his age and they worked well together. Under the tutelage of DeQuille and Goodman, Clemens learned the basics of good reporting, and likewise of good editing. Here he freely honed his imagination and his literary skills.

When Clemens found genuine news to be lacking, he simply manufactured his own. Once he created a graphic story of a miner who massacred his entire family. Most subscribers believed the story and were upset to learn it was one of his fabrications. No one on staff had attempted to pull the story, thinking that Clemens' lively writing kept readers interested and gained new subscribers.

Clemens' being the brother of the Secretary of the Territory, may have held influence in Goodman's decision to hire him. When the legislative session convened in the fall of 1862, Clemens was dispatched to Carson City to cover the events. By this time, Mollie and Jennie had arrived and their home became a center for balls and receptions, where Clemens became well known as a storyteller and parlor entertainer.

Clemens developed a jesting feud with a reporter named Clement Rice from the rival paper, the *Virginia City Daily Union*. Dubbing Rice "the Unreliable" he poked fun at the reporter while giving himself the name "Reliable." The fictional conflict, while a spoof, became a technique Clemens would use often in his later writings.

In 1863, Clemens wrote a few pieces and signed them "Mark Twain," taken from the call of the leadsman on the river. The idea, though quite small and insignificant at the time, would be the birth of one of the most well known names in American history. Because the newspapers distributed stories and articles to other papers, Clemens found he had a following all up and down the western seaboard, in addition to most of Nevada. Soon even his friends were calling him Mark instead of Sam.

Writing to his mother—less often now than before—he bragged about his fame. "Everybody knows me, and I fare like a prince wherever I go, be it on this side of the mountains or the other. And I am proud to say I am the most conceited ass in the Territory."

His reference to the "other" side of the mountains referred to a short trip he made to San Francisco with Clement Rice. He found the city much to his liking. Meeting with some of the literary folk of the city, he found his fame had preceded him. He visited the offices of the *Golden Era* and the *San Francisco Daily Morning Call*, the former a true literary paper, the latter a cheap but popular newspaper. As a smart newspaperman, Clemens, now assuming the pen name Mark Twain, made deals to write for both.

Yet another incident had great impact on Twain while he lived in Nevada. A well-known humorist by the name of Artemus Ward showed up in Virginia City on a lecture tour. Being a writer as well, Ward spent a great deal of time at the offices of the *Enterprise* helping write the paper and visiting with the staff after hours. Twain and Ward became quick friends. Studying Ward closely, Twain watched for clues to his great success.

When Ward left for the next leg of his tour, he encouraged Mark Twain not to stay in Nevada, but to come to New York, where his talents would be more appreciated. While Twain wasn't ready to relocate yet, he began to submit his work back East and had an article published in the New York *Sunday Mercury*. The idea of greater fame, however, remained securely planted in Twain's mind.

January 1864 found Twain once again in Carson City to cover the legislature in session. Just a few days after his arrival, his niece Jennie became ill and died of meningitis. The death was a blow to family and friends alike. While Twain wanted to help his brother through the grief, he still could not tolerate being around Orion for more than a few days at a time. His brother's constant attempts at fathering Twain irritated him and drove him further away.

Venting his feelings the only way he knew how, Twain channeled his anger into his writing. In an article appearing in the *Enterprise*, he lambasted local undertakers for profiteering on the grief of others.

In spite of all the good things that happened to Twain in Nevada, restlessness began to bother him. Whether consciously or unconsciously, he allowed events to happen which ensured his departure. In his usual lampooning style, he accused some of the leading women of Carson City of contributing money to a miscegenation society, a group that promotes marriage and cohabitation between races. In reality, they were raising money for the United States Sanitary Commission, a national agency assisting the Civil War sick and wounded. Writing when he was inebriated one evening, he later said he did not intend for the joke to be printed, but that it had been accidentally picked up for the paper.

The women of Carson City and the rival newspaper protested. At the same time, Twain had accused the employees of the *Union* of reneging on their pledges to the commission. The issues became heated and blown out of proportion, resulting in challenges to a duel for Mark Twain. While such a challenge may seem an extreme measure, duels were commonly used as a method of justice in the Wild West. Finally, Twain decided to leave town on the next stagecoach. While he would later say he left to avoid prosecution, it would seem more likely that he left to avoid embarrassment. Mark Twain, the Washoe Giant, the Wild Humorist of the Pacific Slope, was gone. His presence would be sorely missed by many in Virginia City.

Arriving in San Francisco in May 1864, he started working immediately as a reporter for the *Call*. For Twain, accustomed to the fun of the *Enterprise*, the work was unbearably dull and boring. One day when he saw one of the many Chinese immigrants being brutalized by a San Francisco local, Twain wrote about it in a heated article. His editor, however, refused to print such a thing, saying the paper had to respect the prejudices of their readers. Twain didn't have the same authority in San Francisco as he did in Virginia City. He quit the *Call* after working there for four months.

Looking for other markets for his writing, he turned to a new literary weekly, *The Californian*. Started by another writer named Bret Harte, the magazine paid liberally, but not on a regular basis. Competition among writers was more intense in San Francisco and caused Twain to suffer from deep-seated feelings of defeat and failure. A crash in the stock market made the few mining stocks he still held worthless, and silver production was steadily declining. The mining bonanza was nearly over. Each day put Twain deeper in debt and deeper into depression.

Feeling the need to get away, Twain left for a place called Jackass Hill and the cabin of his close friend's brother. Jim Gillis lived in the mountains not to mine for gold, but for the peace and beauty of the area. Twain spent 12 weeks in the hills, watching other men mining for gold and listening to their tales around the campfires at night. Keeping close notes of all that was said, he thought more and more about the persona of Mark Twain.

One story he heard caught his attention. A man named Coleman told a tale about a bet on a jumping frog. When Twain returned to San Francisco, he worked on breathing new life into the story. The long Civil War ended a month after Twain returned to town, but he made no mention of it in his notes or his journal. He was far removed from such events.

Still in need of funds, he agreed to become a roving reporter for the *Enterprise*. Joe Goodman offered to pay him $100 for the work, funds which would help to bail him out of debt. But the writing proved tedious and tiresome. At the point when Twain felt the most depressed, his jumping frog story was picked up by New York's *Saturday Press*. While it could do little for his debts, it gave him the needed splash of fame and bolstered his confidence.

At a time when Twain needed money more than he ever had in his life, he received word that Orion was negotiating to sell the family land in Tennessee for $200,000. However, when Orion learned that the purchaser planned to turn the land into a wine vineyard, Orion's belief in strict temperance caused him to squelch the deal. Twain was furious. Not only did the land deal affect him, but it would also have helped his mother and Pamela, who was now a widow. He determined not to write to his brother for a year.

Wanting desperately to get away, he made a deal with the *Sacramento Union* to be their reporter in the Sandwich Islands, which later became Hawaii. The development of the sugar industry on the islands made it a place of great interest to Americans. On March 7, 1866, Twain boarded the *Ajax* and sadly sailed out of the Golden Gate city, not knowing where life was taking him.

MARK TWAIN, AUTHOR

The newly established writer Mark Twain wasted no time starting to work on his new post, writing letters back to the *Union* before ever reaching the shore of the islands. Harking back to the spoof-writing Twain had done using Unreliable and Reliable, he created a character with whom he could counterbalance in his travel writings. Calling him simply Brown, Twain used the fabricated character to be the reactionary while Mark Twain held the role of the one who looked for the nobler aspects of the place.

Once arriving in Honolulu, Twain visited the offices of the *Pacific Commercial Advertiser*. Here he made needed contacts for travel and for procuring information. Introduced to the king's grand chamberlain, and later the king himself, Twain enjoyed a social dinner with the royalty of the islands. Having grown up around slaves, Twain expressed amazement that the dark-skinned people of the islands held positions of political power and responsibility and that they enjoyed self-rule. Some he said, were "almost as dark as negroes." The conflict between what he'd learned as a child and these new experiences is clear in his writing, when he occasionally referred to the natives as "savages." And yet he met, talked, and ate with them as equals.

Not all of his important contacts were with the natives; Twain was fortunate to meet two American diplomats. One, Anson Burlingame, liked Twain and took time from his busy schedule to talk and share advice. Burlingame advised him to stop spending time with inferior men and to associate with men of superior intellect and character. Twain would eventually heed this good advice.

Twain's original plan to see the islands in six weeks quickly changed—it would take much longer. Travel in the islands was primitive at best, and there was much more to see and learn than he'd been told. The islands offered sights Twain had never dreamed of—palm trees, thick jungles, exotic plants, beautiful tropical flowers, lovely dark-skinned natives, and fiery-hot live volcanoes. Ever the adventurer, Twain had to see the crater of the volcano up close, witnessing firsthand the glowing hot molten lava issuing forth plumes of steam and dark smoke. Everything he saw found its way into the letters sent back to the states in accounts that proved to be humorous and entertaining as well as informative.

Gathering information on the sugar industry, Twain rode horseback from plantation to plantation across the island of Hawaii. Never having been a good horseman, he suffered terribly from saddle sores.

In an incredible stroke of luck, before returning home, he happened upon an incredible story. Survivors of a shipwreck, who had lasted 43 days in open lifeboats, had washed up on the shore of Hawaii. Burlingame brought word of it to Twain, who went to the rescue site and interviewed the survivors. The story made the front page of the *Union*, and from there reached newspapers across the country.

After a stay of five months, Twain returned home to the large debts he'd left behind. He missed the quiet of the islands and often wished he had never left. "Home again. No—*not* home again—in prison again—and all the wild sense of freedom gone. The city seems so cramped, and so dreary with toil and care and business anxiety."

While writing the last remaining letters due to the *Sacramento Union*, Twain thought of using his travel material for a lecture. Lecturers, he knew, made more income than writers. He rented a hall and designed humorous handbills for distribution in the city. The humorous tagline at the bottom hinted at his doubts whether anyone would come: "Doors open at 7 o'clock. The trouble begins at 8 o'clock."

When Twain delivered his lecture to a hall filled with attentive listeners who laughed uproariously at his jokes, he knew he discovered a niche. He hired a friend to be his stage manager and advance man. A tour was arranged that took him first to Sacramento, then back to Nevada. It even included his old stomping grounds in Virginia City.

Twain worried about his reception in his home city, but all of his old friends received him with enthusiasm and bragged that Mark Twain got his start right there in Virginia City. Even in Carson City, where Twain had so thoughtlessly insulted the key ladies of the town, the reception was nothing but warm and hearty. However, meeting with old friends reminded him of Burlingame's advice to try and improve his social status.

Back in San Francisco, good fortune smiled on Twain when the prestigious newspaper *Alta California* offered to pay his traveling expenses if he would be their roving reporter. Twain immediately made plans to leave California and travel back East. Instead of going overland, he traveled by boat, stopping to cross Central America by train and catching a boat on the other side.

The first leg of his journey aboard the steamer *America* proved to be a delight—in spite of hurricane weather—because of Captain Ned Wakeman. The lively captain kept Twain entertained with amusing yarns, which included incorrigible grammar and the latest of swear words. On the Atlantic side of the Isthmus of Panama, Twain boarded a steamer, the *San Francisco*. Only two days at sea, the dreaded disease cholera surfaced, terrorizing everyone aboard. Day after day, sheet-wrapped corpses were buried at sea. It was a deeply grateful Mark Twain who stepped off the ship in New York City on January 12, 1867.

Twain wasted no time in making contacts with newspapers and with people he knew who moved east, such as Charles Henry Webb. Infused with new determination, he set about on several fronts to make Mark Twain a success. Webb agreed to help Twain release a collection of his stories, with Webb acting as the editor and publisher. With the book secured, Twain submitted short pieces that found their way into print in substantial magazines. At the same time he lined up key people to help him organize a lecture tour. A man named Frank Fuller became his agent in charge of the lecture circuit.

Attending the wealthy Plymouth Church in Brooklyn, Twain met Henry Ward Beecher and learned about an upcoming trip with selected church members to Europe and the Holy Land. Twain knew instantly he wanted to take part in the trip too. Putting down his deposit for the journey, he wrote to his editors at the *Alta* to negotiate a deal with them. If they paid his way, he would submit two letters a week rather than only one. They agreed.

Before leaving the country, Twain made a trip home to see his mother, now 64, and Pamela and her two children, Annie and Sammy. Visiting old haunts, Twain gave lectures to raise money and received great hometown acclaim. More than five years had passed since he'd left Hannibal, and he was disappointed to see how the economy of the town had faltered. The end of the steamboat trade resulted in a financial depression. Many of Twain's friends were married with families, many had moved away, and still others had died or been killed in the Civil War. It was a bittersweet visit.

Returning to the East Coast, Twain made his lecture debut in Washington, D.C., on the very day that word came of the death of Artemus Ward. While the news saddened Twain, it also gave new impetus to his act. He would now step into the void left by Ward.

The *Quaker City* left New York on June 6, 1867, with Twain aboard. This trip across the Atlantic would become the first of many for him. Passengers, made up mostly of clergy and religious folk, stood in stark contrast to the company to which Twain was accustomed. They forbade dancing and poker was banned and replaced with more respectable card games. While their staid behavior at first only irritated Twain, eventually it angered him immensely. It would be a long trip. He worked out his anger by poking fun at his shipmates in the letters he wrote for the paper.

There were, however, a few people with whom Twain could have a good time. A few men whom he dubbed the "smoking room set," allowed him to be himself for short periods of time. Mary Mason Fairbanks, wife of the *Cleveland Herald* publisher, became a good friend to Twain by editing his work and assisting him with his writing. He took her advice when she told him to stop using too much slang and bad grammar. Seven years her junior, Twain called her Mother Fairbanks. The two would become lifelong friends.

In addition to writing for the *Alta*, Twain had made agreements with the *New York Herald* and the *New York Tribune* as well. For his travel writing, he resurrected his imaginary sidekick named Brown, to whom he attributed the cruder jokes. Comparable to his writings from Hawaii, Twain's letters were full of humorous out-of-the-ordinary insights into the people and places along the way. He developed a talent for seeking out intriguing little details, whether about the costumes, the customs, or the money systems encountered at each stop.

After a short stay in the Azores, the steamer headed for the Strait of Gibraltar. From there, Twain and the smoking set separated from the group and made their way to Tangiers. The wild life in Islamic Africa fascinated Twain because it was so thoroughly foreign. He and his friends purchased flowing robes, fezzes, and yellow slippers, then wore them to the shipboard Fourth-of-July ball.

On several occasions Twain and his friends remained separated from the rest of the group; one of these times included their tour of Italy. Before leaving Italy, they visited Vesuvius, an active volcano. Comparing it to the ones he had seen in Hawaii, Twain described Vesuvius as looking more like a ditch. During the tour of Italy, Twain received word that he'd been offered a job as the private secretary to Nevada Senator William Stewart. The offer pleased him. It would allow him to earn a good salary and possibly find a government position for Orion. The job would be easier than writing or lecturing.

In Greece, Twain was particularly entranced with the vast excavations taking place there. The thought that so many artifacts from past civilizations could be hidden beneath the ground amazed him. Comparing the other sights he'd seen, he wrote, "It is a world of precious relics, a wilderness of marred and mutilated gems, and yet what are these things to the wonders that lie buried here under the ground?"

Another source of fascination for Twain was discovering and meeting highly educated, well-mannered, well-dressed black persons. One such man served as the Moroccan consul to Gibraltar; another happened to be their guide in Venice. The guide had come from South Carolina, where his parents were slaves. He could speak four languages and knew more about Venice than any other guide in the city. About him, Twain wrote, "He dresses better than any of us, I think, and is daintily polite. Negroes are deemed as good as white people in Venice, and so this man feels no desire to go back to his native land. His judgment is correct."

At one point during the trip, Twain happened to be spending time with a young 17-year-old boy named Charles Jervis Langdon, the son of a rich coal merchant from Elmira, New York. While the two were in conversation, Charlie showed Twain a miniature portrait of his 22-year-old sister, Olivia. Twain was smitten by the beauty in the photograph and afterward asked to see it often, once even asking Charlie to give it to him, but the boy refused. Twain resolved that one day he would meet the girl in the photograph.

Of all the sites Twain visited on this trip, he was the most disappointed with the Holy Lands. While still in Damascus, he caught an intestinal illness that slowed him down and made him even more irritable. Riding horses through the desert heat made things even worse. By the time he arrived in Palestine, he was not in good humor. In Jerusalem, he was more than a little repulsed by the "rags, wretchedness, poverty, and dirt," as well as the masses of malformed and diseased people. How this land could enamor Christians was beyond his comprehension.

Arriving in Egypt, Twain learned that he was behind in his correspondence, which was upsetting enough. Worse still, he learned that some of his letters had failed to reach the United States. Back on board ship with the passengers he loathed, an exhausted Twain wrote furiously to catch up his work. A cholera scare cancelled several of the final stops, cutting the cruise short, which was fine with Twain who couldn't wait to get home and away from his shipmates. "Well, perhaps it was a pleasure excursion, but it certainly did not look like one; certainly it did not act like one," he wrote to the *Herald*. "The pleasure ship was a synagogue, and the pleasure trip was a funeral excursion without a corpse."

Upon arriving in New York, Twain couldn't wait to put distance between him and those with whom he'd traveled for so many months. He hurried to Washington, D.C., to become a part of the political scene.

MARK TWAIN: FAMILY MAN

Mark Twain informed Frank Fuller that he preferred to wait before setting up lectures featuring highlights from his overseas trip. He wanted his lectures to stand alone and not be thought of in conjunction with the fame of the *Quaker City*.

Hurrying off to the nation's capital, Twain was ready to become involved in politics and make important contacts in high places. In his position as assistant to Senator Stewart, Twain often sat in proxy for the senator in important meetings, even signing the senator's name to certain documents.

Twain's observations from the capital found their way into a newsletter of his own creation, as well as newspaper articles contributed to the *Tribune* and *Herald* in New York and other papers out West. He was delighted to learn that "hobnobbing with these old Generals and Senators and other humbugs" made great copy.

The foray into politics, however, did not last. Twain and the senator had a falling out that caused Twain to resign after less than a month. Joking about the incident, as he did about everything in life, he wrote that Stewart yelled at him, "'Leave the House! Leave it forever and forever, too!,' [I] regarded that as a sort of covert intimation that my services would be dispensed with, and so I resigned."

Following the resignation, and now without a means of income, Twain regretted not allowing Fuller to line up a series of lectures. His fame had spread because of the letters from his tour and subsequent articles after his arrival home. Bewildering choices lay before him. He wasn't sure whether to be a roving diplomat, a committed writer, or a speaker becoming rich on the lecture circuit.

One thing was not uncertain—he had a standing invitation from Charlie Langdon to visit the family. He learned they were in New York over the holidays, so Twain made it a point to visit. Meeting Olivia Langdon for the first time was no disappointment for him. "She was slender and beautiful and girlish—and she was both girl and woman." Later he would add, "She remained both girl and woman to the last day of her life." Twain attended a Charles Dickens reading with the family on New Year's Eve. The next day, he arrived at their hotel suite and, neglecting all his other calls for the day, stayed with them until midnight.

The Langdon family, Twain knew, was far superior to him in class and social status. While Olivia's father, Jervis, made a fortune in coal, the family was unlike most other capitalists. During the Civil War, as committed abolitionists, their home was used as one of the stops for the Underground Railroad. Black abolitionist leader Frederick Douglass spent time in their home as a welcome visitor.

Langdon money supported a female college, which academically compared favorably with male colleges. Jervis Langdon held progressive views about management and labor, views that promoted peaceful working relationships in his business. On top of all that, the Langdon family, members of a local church they had founded, sang hymns and prayed together. No one in the family smoked or drank alcohol, and they were unlike any family Twain had ever met in his life.

In addition to her younger brother Charlie, Olivia had an older sister, Susan, whose husband Theodore Crane worked for Jervis as his financial manager. Livy, as Olivia was called by her friends, suffered from health problems resulting from a fall while ice skating several years earlier. The accident had at one time left her partially paralyzed. Her health was greatly improved by the time she met Twain. Olivia's father, being past 60, longed to see his daughter married and cared for. Jervis liked what he saw in Twain, even if the young writer was a bit rough around the edges.

After this first visit, Twain parted by promising to visit them at their home in Elmira as soon as possible. Other pressing needs kept that from happening for another eight months.

Twain's fame brought him book offers, but having been disappointed in the sales of his first book, he determined to be more cautious and wise. In a letter to his mother, he wrote, "I had my mind made up to *one* thing. I wasn't going to touch a book unless there was *money* in it, and a good deal of it."

Turning down an offer for a flat fee of several thousand dollars, Twain chose to go with book royalties. He contracted with Elisha Bliss of the American Publishing Company, whose company sold books by subscription—door-to-door sales—a practice scorned by most of the literary world. But of course the profit margin for the author greatly increased.

Scheduling a lecture tour at the same time he began working on the book, Twain's days were busier than ever. Although lecturing paid extremely well, it was a hard life. The hotels of Twain's day were often dirty and shabby, with lumpy beds, terrible food, and poor or no service. If he stayed in the home of a local, he found they wanted to show him every site in the city from the cemetery to the courthouse. For that reason he often preferred the poor hotel room—where he could smoke cigars and write—to the soft bed of someone's guestroom.

In March 1868, Twain received devastating news from the *Alta*. Feeling they had full rights to the letters Twain had written for the paper, they were going to use them for a book, which would supercede Twain's book release. Panicked, Twain took the first steamer out of New York heading for San Francisco. Bliss, whose interests were involved as well, loaned Twain the money for the trip.

Back in the Golden Gate city, Twain was greeted like a conquering hero and he immediately took in a good deal of money lecturing. After smoothing out the misunderstanding with the editors at *Alta*, who now doubted a book would even be profitable for them, Twain began work on the book that would become *The Innocents Abroad*. Writing through the long night hours, he finished the manuscript in six weeks. He wrote to "Mother" Fairbanks, telling her he wished she were on hand to help with the editing. Instead, he turned to his old friend, Bret Harte, who helped Twain choose what to omit. In one piece of good advice, Harte told him to leave the boorish Brown out of the writing altogether and use the pen name Mark Twain for all the insights. Twain did exactly that and created a strong book attributed only to his famous pen name.

When time came for Twain to leave the West Coast, his fame was so great the steamboat company gave him a free trip home.

Upon delivering the manuscript to Bliss back in New York, Twain traveled to Elmira to spend time with the Langdon family. Staying at the lavish Langdon home for two weeks, Twain found he was more taken with Olivia than before. Before leaving, he asked for her hand in marriage, but she turned down his proposal, which was the accepted mode of formality for a modest lady at this time. He wrote love letters to Olivia while on his lecture tour in an attempt to win her hand. Olivia wrote back and gave to him her pet name of "Youth," a nickname she would use throughout their years together. Through scores of letters their romance blossomed.

Twain worried about his forthcoming book and subsequent tour. But most of all he worried about becoming a married man. Jervis Langdon wanted someone for his daughter who would settle in one place. Not only was Twain unsettled, he was also without the means to support Olivia in a manner to which she was accustomed. Much then depended on his new ventures.

Twain's plan was to lecture using excerpts from his upcoming book—a bit of promotional genius invented by Twain, but which would be copied by authors for years to come. Starting the tour in Cleveland in November 1868 put Twain in close proximity to Mother Fairbanks. Fairbanks assisted Twain in editing the lecture, then attended and wrote a favorable review to place in her husband's newspaper. She stated that Mark Twain had "conclusively proved that a man may be a humorist without being a clown. He has elevated the profession by his graceful delivery and by recognizing in his audience something higher than merely a desire to laugh."

While Mary Fairbanks wrote the review as Twain's friend, every word was true. Twain had a natural talent of walking on the stage as though he were walking across "his front yard" and to speak to thousands "as though carrying on a conversation with his neighbor," which his audiences loved.

This success helped to impress the Langdons, and Olivia in particular. Before the tour finished, she was ready to say yes to Twain, and Jervis pronounced his blessing on the union. In his letters, Twain even purported to be serious about Christianity. This, however, was merely a desperate attempt to please Olivia and the family; it would not and could not last.

The two were engaged on February 4, 1869, and Twain began looking for a newspaper to purchase so he could settle down as his new father-in-law expected. He looked at the *Cleveland Herald* and the *Hartford Courant*; negotiations, however, stalled with each. Eventually, with the help of Jervis Langdon, Twain purchased part interest in the *Buffalo Express*, in spite of the fact that he had no desire to live in Buffalo, New York.

Meanwhile Olivia helped Twain with the proofs of his new book, for which she suggested the title, *The Innocents Abroad*. Delays on the book's release both angered and frustrated Twain. While waiting he spent time in Buffalo immersing himself into newspaper work, a world with which he was intimately acquainted. When *Innocents* at last made its appearance, it was an instant success. Post-Civil War America was coming into its own as a wealthy industrial nation and relished the opportunity to poke fun at the Old World. Twain had done just that by satirizing blind reverence to ancient history. The book sold 30,000 copies in the first six months.

Of the rave reviews that accumulated for the book, Twain prized most the one written by William Dean Howells of the elite magazine, the *Atlantic Monthly*. At this point in Twain's life he held the *Atlantic* in great awe, and in later years he would become close friends with William Howells.

As the wedding date of February 2, 1870 approached, Twain and Olivia worked out a housekeeping budget and last-minute details about their life together. Olivia was particularly concerned about Twain's habit of smoking cigars and preached against it in her many letters. Twain responded:

> I shall treat smoking just exactly as I would treat the forefinger of my left hand: If you asked me in all seriousness to cut that finger off, and I saw that you really meant it, & believed that the finger marred my well-being in some mysterious way, and it was plain to me that you could not be entirely satisfied and happy while it remained, I give you my word that I would cut it off.

Surely the prim and proper Miss Olivia had met her match; Twain would never stop smoking cigars.

What was originally planned as a small ceremony at midday grew to be an evening event attended by more than 200 guests. Pamela and Annie, Twain's sister and niece, came for the wedding, feeling much out of place in a gathering of wealthy people surrounded by such opulence. Following the ceremony, a series of surprises was in store for the new bride and groom. Jervis Langdon had arranged for a private railroad car to transport the newlyweds back to Buffalo. Once they arrived in Buffalo, Twain and Olivia were taken by sleigh to a beautifully furnished, three-story brick home which, Twain learned, now belonged to him. It was yet another gift from his wealthy father-in-law.

Settling down into married life, Twain found himself extremely happy. He set to work at the newspaper and used it to write powerful editorials against the lynching of black people, a practice that was becoming commonplace throughout the South. In addition to his own paper, his fame now allowed him to bring in hefty fees for articles submitted to periodicals and other newspapers.

The peace of their first year together was short-lived as Jervis fell ill with cancer. In the few years that Twain had known his father-in-law, the two had formed a close bond and friendship. When Jervis died, on August 6, 1870, Twain grieved as though it were his own father.

Olivia was now pregnant and her health weakened as she watched over her dying father. After his death, she became bedridden for a time. Olivia's long-time friend, Emma Nye, visited in hopes of cheering her and helping with the household. Instead, Nye fell ill with typhoid fever and died, weighing Olivia with even more grief than before.

When the baby arrived November 7, 1870, he was premature and sickly. They named him Langdon Clemens. A few months after Langdon's birth, Olivia developed typhoid fever. Twain was beside himself, wondering from one day to the next if he might lose his wife and his child, and writing became almost impossible. As soon as Olivia's health permitted, Twain put the house on the market and prepared to move to Elmira, where they could begin to heal again.

Back with family, Olivia regained her health and Twain started writing again. Hiking a mile each day up East Hill to a place called Quarry Farm—once used as Jervis's summer retreat—Twain found he could concentrate as he gazed out over the Chemung River Valley south of the town. This spot became his favorite place and he completed much of his writing here. In the quiet of Quarry Farm, Twain completed a book about his years out West, *Roughing It*. While this book did not sell as well as *Innocents*, its publication convinced Twain that he was indeed an author.

By the following summer, life for the Clemens family had definitely turned around. Olivia, again pregnant, was in excellent health, and Twain prepared to return to the lecture circuit. They were ready now to choose a place where they could settle down together, and decided on Hartford, Connecticut. Not only did Twain love the town, but Olivia also had lifelong friends living there. Renting a house there for a time, they planned to build their own home in an area known as

Nook Farm. Nook Farm's residents were a mix of literary and cultural elite. Twain hoped to become an integral part of the town's culture.

The house they eventually built commanded the attention of the entire town. The balcony resembled a pilothouse and the porch a riverboat deck. Lookouts and gothic turrets afforded a splendid view in all directions. The 19-room house cost more than $120,000 including the price of the five-acre plot of ground. Although built for comfort, Twain did very little writing in the expansive library.

In March, Olivia gave birth to their daughter, Olivia Susan. Called Susy, the baby was much healthier than her older brother Langdon, whose development continued to be painfully slow. The next summer, Langdon died, again sinking Olivia into a deep grief and depression. The young wife and mother had experienced three deaths of those near to her in the space of three years.

Only seven weeks after Langdon's death, Twain announced he was traveling to England. In the days before the protection of international copyright laws, literary materials were pirated in other countries working to undercut the author's income on their own works. It was Twain's intention to prevent such things from happening to his books. While this may have been part of the reason for his departure, the full reason may have been that Olivia's grief and sorrow were more than Twain could bear.

SUCCESSES AND FAILURES

The reception Twain received in England both surprised and pleased him. For years Americans had held British authors in high esteem; rarely had the reverse been true. Twain heralded the beginning of a new respect for American writers in England. Artemus Ward, to some degree, paved the way, since all of England admired his New World wit, gathering by the hundreds to fill his lecture halls. Because Ward died in the first bloom of his fame, Twain easily took up Ward's mantle and then improved upon it.

Twain's books, reproduced without permission by two separate publishers, Routledge and Hotten, had sold thousands of copies; this ensuring his fame. However, when the British discovered that Mark Twain was as witty and funny in person, they were overjoyed. Newspapers hung on his every word and rushed to print each funny comment he uttered.

In publisher negotiations, Twain reached an agreement with Routledge only. John Camden Hotten refused to cooperate with Twain, preferring to copy existing works and publishing them at will, without paying royalties. George Routledge, on the other hand, not only entered into a business agreement with Twain, but also took him about town to introduce him to the upper echelons of society. One dinner engagement with a fox-hunting squire, he told Livy in a letter, "had all the seeming of hob-nobbing with the Black Prince in the flesh!—for this fellow is of princely presence & manners, & 35 years old."

News of Twain's popularity in England found its way into the press back home, which in turn caused many to reconsider the value of Mark Twain—especially those in literary circles who thought of Twain as part buffoon, part frontier bumpkin. Mary Fairbanks seemed extraordinarily proud. In a letter, she wrote, "They are treating you handsomely in England—we are glad—everybody is watching you here—and I your anxious Mother am stretching my neck over all the great audience."

In addition to being the star at gala events, Twain took time to attempt to master the German language and to study English history, both of which fascinated him. He became proficient at speaking German, and gathered ideas for possible novels set in medieval England.

Twain's time away had allowed Olivia to hone her own social skills. By the time Twain returned home, Olivia was much improved and had gained many friends in Hartford, one of whom was a lady named Lily Warner. Lily and her husband, Charles Dudley Warner, soon were spending a good deal of time with the Clemenses. One evening when the four were together, the men poked fun at the trite novels their wives read. Olivia and Lily challenged their husbands to write one better. The men accepted the challenge.

Twain threw himself into the work, thoroughly enjoying the plotting process. The finished product, entitled *The Gilded Age*, became an immediate success. It sold out three printings in the first month. The title of the book grew to be a byword for the political and economic graft and corruption of the times.

Traveling to England once again to protect copyrights of the book, he took Olivia and Susy along. Olivia, however, was too homesick to enjoy the trip. Their house was still under construction and she wanted to be on hand to oversee the details. While they were away, what would be referred to as the Panic of 1873 occurred in the United States. The economic disaster gave the Clemenses cause for many sleepless nights. Twain immediately turned his mind to lectures, which is what he always did when money became tight.

The thought of enduring a longer tour made Olivia even more homesick. Twain accompanied her home, stayed for a few days and returned to England to complete his tour. Upon this separation from his wife, Twain felt his deep love for her more keenly than ever before. His letters to her are especially touching, admitting that he wasn't always as open as he should have been. "I am not demonstrative, except at intervals—but I *always* love you—always admire you—am always your champion."

By the summer of 1874, with the expected arrival of another baby, Twain took his family back to Elmira. A tradition had been established of spending summers at Quarry Farm. Sue Crane, Olivia's sister, had commissioned a special study to be built for her famous brother-in-law. The octagonal gazebo, with windows on every side, provided the perfect spot for Twain's writing. The Cranes' open hospitality and love for Twain played a great part in the amount of writing produced by Mark Twain.

Clara Clemens made her way into the world on June 8, 1874. Because Susy couldn't quite say, "baby," Clara's nickname became "Bay"; Twain's family was growing.

While *The Gilded Age* took the nation by storm, it was also made into a stage play, which surpassed the success of the book. Twain received high acclaim and bolstered his income with royalty checks for every performance.

His acceptance into literary circles became guaranteed when he wrote seven installments of articles called "Old Times on the Mississippi" for the *Atlantic*. Letting his memories return to his roots revived a story idea Twain had been mulling over for years—the story of a boy who lives in a Mississippi River town. After writing the book, *The Adventures of Tom Sawyer*, he wasn't sure how to proceed with it. Was it a children's book or an adult book? Exasperated, Twain turned to his friend William Dean Howells for advice. After reading the book, Howells was exuberant in his praise, saying that it was without a doubt a book for children. "I think you ought to treat it explicitly as a boy's story ... if you should put it forth as a study of boy character from the grown-up point of view you give the wrong key to it." Livy agreed with the appraisal, and immensely grateful, Twain followed their advice.

Because of publisher delays, sales for the book were slow and less than Twain had expected. The income from the book became more important as the cost of living for the Clemenses soared. The upkeep of the large house and staff commanded huge sums of money. In addition, Twain's interest and fascination in new innovations and inventions lured him into making unwise investments. Again, because of money, he attempted to write several plays, no doubt recalling the financial success of the dramatization of *The Gilded Age*. None of his subsequent plays came near to matching that success.

Twain wrote for three months out of the year and entertained the remaining nine months, a pattern he would later regret. Life in Hartford consisted of one social event after another, which weighted on both Twain and Olivia. His fame brought scores of letters, most of which he attempted to answer. Some were pleas for help and advice; some just wanted an autograph. While it was the life and status Twain had hoped for and dreamed of, after he attained it, it soon lost its appeal.

Having strived for so long to make a positive impression on Boston's literary elite, Twain nearly erased it all in one evening. Giving a talk at a dinner honoring poet John Greenleaf Whittier and having been invited by Howells, Twain's bawdy humor went awry. Present were Henry Wadsworth Longfellow, Oliver Wendell Holmes, and Ralph Waldo Emerson, all of whose names Twain invoked in relating a story to the audience about an old miner. When no one laughed, Twain was mortified. While Howells supported Twain and did not judge him harshly for the blunder, Twain began to struggle between the identities of Samuel Clemens and Mark Twain. He sent apologies to each of the men in separate letters.

In April 1878, the Clemenses closed their big house, crated the furniture and embarked to Europe for 16 months. On this trip, Olivia did not become as homesick; it was a relief to be away from so many responsibilities. At one time, Olivia had lamented to her mother the problems of running such a large household.

> In this day women must be everything, they must keep up with all the current literature, they must know all about art, they must help in one or two benevolent societies—they must be perfect mothers—they must be perfect housekeepers and graceful, gracious hostesses, they must

know how to give perfect dinners, they must go and visit all the people in the town where they live, they must always be ready to receive their acquaintances—they must dress themselves and their children becomingly and above all they must make their houses "charming" & so on without end— then if they are not studying something their case is a hopeless one.

Olivia failed to mention that she also worked hard at being the editor of all Twain's writings, and would eventually be the teacher for their children. Facing those kinds of daily pressures, it is easy to see why such a trip would be appreciated.

When the family returned home, Twain had acquired enough material for a book he entitled *A Tramp Abroad*. As soon as the book was completed and delivered to the printer, Twain returned to another novel he had started previously. The plot concerned a crown prince who found he looked much like a penniless pauper boy he met. The two decided to change places, after which the young prince became a victim of the harsh laws of the land. Calling it *The Prince and the Pauper*, Twain enjoyed the writing of it as much as anything he'd ever done.

Another daughter graced the household in July 1880. Named Jane Lampton Clemens, she would be called Jean. While she appeared to be the healthy at birth, she would suffer from health problems most of her life.

Twain's *Tramp* book sold well, but life in Hartford continued to be extremely expensive. Twain sunk money into inventions such as a self-pasting scrapbook and adjustable straps for clothing. He dreamed up a game for children to help with memorization, but the resulting product proved to be so complicated no child could understand it. The inventions that captured Twain's attention were those that improved on existing technology, such as a movable typesetter called a compositor, which Twain invested thousands of dollars in through the years. Inventions that introduced entirely new concepts were beyond his comprehension.

When an inventor approached Twain about the possibility of sending the human voice over an electric wire, Twain showed no interest at all. Even when offered all the stock he wanted for only $500, Twain refused. The inventor, Alexander Graham Bell, went on to make a fortune with the telephone. In fact, Twain would later install one of the first telephones of Hartford in his home.

Elisha Bliss, who had been Twain's publisher from the outset, died on September 28, 1880. While he had not always been fair to Twain, and had failed to properly protect copyrights, Bliss and the American Publishing Company played a large part in building the fame and success that Twain enjoyed. After Bliss' death, Twain made the decision to become his own publisher; he soon found that publishing was not easy, and he had no concept of how much work it involved. But then, Twain never had good business sense, and he was terribly gullible. Time and again, he would be taken advantage of in financial matters, costing him dearly.

In the spring of 1882, Twain prepared to take a trip down the Mississippi River as research for his new book. With him, he had a new machine called a typewriter. As one who loved gadgets, he spent much of his spare time practicing typing.

Twain found the river had changed drastically since his childhood days. The federal government had altered the flow of the river, marking channels with buoys and shoring up unstable banks. Traffic signals directed the pilot along the way. For Twain, the glory had faded and the thrill of navigating through uncertain waters no longer existed. One pilot, Twain said, recognized him after 21 years. The nostalgic journey presented Twain with a mixture of delight and dismay. "The romance of boating is gone," he wrote home to Olivia. "In Hannibal the steamboat man is no longer a god. The youth don't talk river slang any more. Their pride is apparently railroads"....

Back home, Twain began entrusting more of his business matters to his nephew, Charley Webster. Charley, the husband of Pamela's daughter, Annie, assumed the responsibility of investing Twain's money. The first stock Charley invested in, the Independent Watch Company, was fraudulent. Orion told Twain that Webster knew the company was a fraud, but sold the stocks to family members anyway. Since Twain and Orion had never been particularly close, Twain felt more inclined to give Charley the benefit of the doubt, a decision that would return to haunt him. Such losses never seemed to faze Twain anyway. As he wrote to his friends the Howells, "I must speculate in something, such being my nature."

Life on the Mississippi was not a labor of love for Twain. While his travel books earned him a decent income, they could never satisfy his creative bent. He could only free his imagination by writing creative fiction. Twain often had two or three projects under composition at the same time. Tiring of one—or becoming discouraged with it—he simply switched to another.

The summer of 1884 was again spent at Quarry Farm, and Twain worked on a novel about a poor white boy who meets and travels with a slave seeking freedom. Set in the mid 1800s, the story is entirely told from the boy's point of view, in his Southern dialect and slang. The book would earn Mark Twain the acclaim of being anointed the father of the American novel. Twain had no idea his book would be considered a masterpiece; he only knew that he thoroughly enjoyed working on it, offering him the opportunity to speak out against slavery, violence, and bigotry.

Huckleberry Finn became a success in both America and England in spite of the fact that some librarians and critics deemed it vulgar and unfit for young readers.

Throughout the 1880's, Twain continued to invest money into the Paige typesetter. James Paige convinced Twain that when finished and marketed, the compositor would earn millions. However, Paige continually made changes to the machine and never brought it to a point where it could be used and tested. Meanwhile the linotype, while not as innovative as the Paige compositor, was manufactured and placed in newspaper and printing offices. It was continually tested and updated.

By this time Twain and his nephew had developed the Charley Webster Publishing Company, and Twain became a full-fledged publisher. In addition to his own books, Twain became interested in publishing the autobiography of former President Ulysses S. Grant. Grant, suffering from cancer, worked diligently with a stenographer hired by Twain to dictate the book. The revered Civil War general and president died three days after he finished the last of his notes for his memoirs.

Due in part to Twain's understanding of subscription bookselling, Grant's book sold more than 300,000 copies. The profits earned a great deal of money for both Twain and for Grant's widow. The invigorating experience of such success caused Twain to be even more reckless in business deals and in the way he handled money. He continued to invest almost $3,000 a month into the Paige typesetter, in addition to the exorbitant cost of keeping up the large house in Hartford. Charley

Webster continued on as the inept leader of the publishing company, accepting books that had no hope of making a profit.

Ever interested in social justice, Twain created a story about a factory worker who is swept back in a time warp to the days of King Arthur. The book, *A Connecticut Yankee in King Arthur's Court*, dealt with the themes of human rights and social justice, themes which increased Twain's audience even more. His first book in five years, it was released in 1889 and was desperately needed to help rescue him from financial trouble.

In time, evidence was found that a bookkeeper at the publishing house had embezzled a great deal of money. Twain was given reason to believe Charley Webster colluded with the bookkeeper, but he couldn't prove it. By now, Twain was so deeply entangled with Charley and the publishing company that he could not figure out a way to resolve the situation.

In the space of a few short years, a number of tragedies affected Twain and his family. It began with their close friends, the Howells' daughter Winnie, who was only 25 years old when she died suddenly. Olivia's brother-in-law Theodore Crane died in 1889 and a year later, both she and Twain lost their mothers within a month of one another. At the same time their youngest daughter, Jean, suffered from a seizure and was seriously ill. The Paige typesetter venture was on the verge of collapsing, condemning Twain to financial ruin.

In April 1891, the Twain's family closed the Hartford house and embarked for Europe once again. Not only was Twain leaving the country and the embarrassment of his losses, he also intended to turn his back on writing. The family would never again reside at the unique and beautiful home in Nook Farm.

MAKING A COMEBACK

The costs of living in Europe, infinitely cheaper than in America, helped Twain recover financially only a little. Being away from the pressures of home, however, helped the entire family. Clara and Susy became involved in the study of music, while Jean and Olivia received medical treatments that were not available in America. Jean, now diagnosed with epilepsy, feared she would never marry.

Twain's popularity never abated. Because his books were read around the world, he was constantly in demand at royal courts, embassies, and universities. The press followed him incessantly, seeking out bits of his wit and wisdom to quote in the morning papers.

Periodically, Twain made journeys home in an attempt to untangle the mess of affairs he left behind. In 1893, another economic crash hit the country in which all capital withered. Twain inquired of his friends to borrow money but was unsuccessful; that is, until he was introduced to Henry Rogers. Rogers, the mastermind behind the Standard Oil monopoly, had long been an admirer of the writings of Mark Twain. Rogers was more than agreeable to loan the necessary capital and to handle Twain's financial affairs as well. At first Twain wasn't sure whether Rogers was too good to be true, but at the time, he had little choice but to trust him.

Rogers's first step was to try to rescue the Paige typesetter and the publishing business. In a final test of the typesetter, arranged and paid for by Rogers, the machine failed to live up to its potential; it was unable to withstand the rigors of daily use. Because Twain had counted on the success of the typesetter to rescue Webster and Company, now all was lost. Twain was forced to declare bankruptcy—news that made headlines in major newspapers across the country.

Once the worst was over, Twain felt a sense of relief. He was determined that somehow he would pay back every penny to his creditors. However, the knowledge that they could not return to their Hartford home nearly broke his heart.

Twain knew the only way he could make money quickly was to lecture. Plans for a round-the-world lecture tour were soon underway—with Olivia's approval. It was agreed that Jean and Susy would stay with their Aunt Sue, and Clara would accompany her parents on the tour.

Twain found that he was still a viable commodity on the world stage. It was good to know that he had not lost his stage presence or his appeal. After so many negatives in his life, he felt revived. "Lecturing is gymnastics, chest-expander, medicine, mind healer, blues destroyer, all in one," he wrote in a letter to the *San Francisco Examiner*. "I am twice as well as I was when I started out." Twain would turn 60 during this tour. Before the North American leg of his journey was complete, he sent $5,000 in profits to Rogers to apply to his debts.

Their leisurely pace of travel allowed the trio to enjoy the journey. News from home told of Jean's progress in school and that Susy, who had suffered from emotional problems, was settled down and much improved. All looked forward to a reunion soon, and Twain could hardly wait to get back to his writing. When they arrived in England, a telegram arrived with the worst possible news: Susy had contracted spinal meningitis and was deathly ill. The next telegram announced that she had died on August 18, 1896. The family was inconsolable, and Twain blamed himself. Had it not been for his financial problems, the family would have been together and might have been there to help.

Following Susy's funeral and burial, Twain, Olivia, Jean, and Clara moved to England and detached themselves from the world. For a year they celebrated no holidays, nor did they acknowledge birthdays. Twain continued to write about the world tour and created the book *Following the Equator*, which upon publication sold more than 30,000 copies.

By January 1898, Rogers informed Twain that all of his debts were resolved. Twain and Olivia were thrilled—it was the first good news they'd heard in many months. Rogers now determined to make wise investments with Twain's money, something Twain could never do on his own. By the fall of 1900, four years after Susy's death, the Clemens family felt ready to return home. They were prevented from returning to the Hartford house, this time because of the memories. The Clemens family could not bear to live there after Susy's death.

Because Twain had his writing, he could immerse himself in it as a catharsis after Susy's death. Olivia, on the other hand, had no such mode of healing. While Twain began to feel his old vigor returning, Olivia felt aged and weary and began to experience more severe health problems. Two years following their return, Olivia experienced a heart attack, which placed her in mortal danger. Suddenly, nothing mattered to Twain except his beloved wife.

For a time, the doctors refused to allow Twain to see his wife, saying that his presence agitated her. Sometimes he stayed outside her door waiting for the moment he could to go in and see her. He was beginning to realize how important Olivia was to him. On their 33rd wedding anniversary, February 2, 1903, Twain wrote, "It's a long time ago, my darling, but the 33 years have been richly profitable to us, through love—a love which has grown, not diminished, and is worth more each year than it was the year before. And so it will be always, dearest old Sweetheart of my youth."

When the doctors suggested a milder climate for Olivia, Twain immediately thought of Florence, Italy, where they'd lived previously.

He and Jean and Clara arranged the trip, leaving the country in the fall of 1903.

Before their departure, an agreement had been forged between Twain and the Harper Publishing Company. Negotiations led by Henry Rogers wrestled the remaining book copyrights away from Frank Bliss— Elisha's son, who had been reluctant to release them—for the sum of $50,000. The money was split between Twain and Harper. From then on, Harper agreed to pay at least $25,000 a year for the rights to publish all of Twain's future books. This single agreement guaranteed Twain sufficient income for the remainder of his life. In his notebook, he wrote, "The contract signed that day concentrates all my books in Harper's hands, and now at last they are valuable: in fact they are a fortune."

Twain hired a secretary, Isabel Lyon, to accompany them on the trip, along with the Clemens' housekeeper of many years, Katy Leary. After arriving in Italy, Olivia showed measured improvement. Twain began dictating his memoirs to Lyon for an hour each day, a process he greatly enjoyed. He discovered that as he recalled his past, the dividing wall between Samuel Clemens and Mark Twain weakened and began to crumble. In a letter to the Howells he exclaimed that "an Autobiography is the truest of all books; for while it inevitably consists mainly of extinctions of the truth, shirkings of the truth, partial revealments of the truth, with hardly an instance of plain straight truth, the remorseless truth *is* there, between the lines."

Olivia's rally gave the family false hopes for her recovery. Twain even looked for a villa to purchase where they could take up permanent residence. On the evening of June 5, 1904, Olivia asked Twain to play the piano and sing for her the old Negro spirituals as only he could play and sing them. Shortly thereafter, Olivia's heart stopped; Katy Leary had to bring the sad news to Twain that she had died. He had lost his faithful companion of 34 years.

They returned to America, where Olivia was buried in the family plot in Elmira. Writing to his pastor friend Joe Twichell, Twain said about his life with Olivia, "I was richer than any other person in the world, and now I am that pauper without peer."

Without Olivia, the family did not fare well at all. Clara was close to a nervous breakdown and Jean's seizures became more frequent and intense. In his confusion and loneliness, Twain turned to the companionship of Isabel Lyon, his secretary, so much so that rumors of marriage began to spread. Twain quickly acted to squelch the rumors and to ensure the public that Lyon was his secretary only.

In his waning years, Twain continued to write prolifically. In January 1906, he hired Albert Bigelow Paine to become his biographer. He and Paine worked closely together, using a stenographer to record Twain's ramblings and storytelling everyday. Twain also gathered about him a group of young girls whom he referred to as his "angelfish." Still with no grandchildren of his own, Twain wanted to be surrounded with innocence and laughter in his old age.

Three years after Olivia's death, at a time when Twain cared nothing about travel, he received word that he was awarded an honorary degree from Oxford. One last time, the Old Lion packed his steamer trunks and crossed the Atlantic to England, where he was treated like royalty each and every day of his six-week stay.

For the trip, Twain hired a man named Ralph Ashcroft as a secretary and traveling companion. Upon Twain's return, Ashcroft stayed on the payroll and assisted Isabel Lyon with managing Twain's affairs. Jean had been committed to a sanitarium, where her epilepsy could be properly cared for, and Clara sought a singing career in Europe.

Having no place in America to settle down in, Twain contracted to have a house built in Redding, Connecticut, and moved there in June 1908. The townspeople turned out en masse to welcome him, proud to have such a noted celebrity in their midst.

Clara felt a great deal of mistrust toward Lyon and Ashcroft and feared they did not have her father's best interest at heart. In December 1908, she arrived at Redding and vowed to stay by her father's side until she convinced him to have an objective person look over the bookkeeping. When she finally managed to convince him, it was discovered that Lyon had used Twain's assets to more than quadruple her own salary over a period of several years. Twain had been taken advantage of yet again.

During one of her rare visits home, Jean was much improved and found she could stay on as her father's secretary. Biographer Paine also helped manage Twain's affairs. With Ashcroft and Lyon gone, the household became peaceful once again. In the fall the family gathered for the joyous occasion of Clara's marriage to Ossip Gabrilowitsch, after which the newlyweds settled in Europe to live.

In December 1909, Jean happily immersed herself in Christmas preparations, just as her mother used to do. Sadly, just two days before Christmas, Jean suffered a severe seizure in the bathtub, and drowned tragically.

Twain found he could not even mourn the loss of Jean. In fact, he envied her release from the cares of this world. Wanting to escape from his pain, Twain planned a trip to Bermuda, where the pace of life was slower and calmer. His trip to Bermuda was uneventful, but by spring, heart pains plagued him and he had difficulty breathing. Friends of Twain summoned Paine to help escort him home, and Clara was cabled to meet them back in Redding. When she arrived on April 18th her father was still conscious—she was able to tell him the good news of her pregnancy. His last request was to have Clara sing for him at his bedside, which she did.

On Thursday, April 21, 1910, Mark Twain died—a day after Halley's Comet again lent its brilliant light to the sky, just as it had on the day of his birth.

EPILOGUE

Mark Twain's fame extended far beyond his writing talents. Known around the world, Twain elevated the concept of "celebrity" to a new level, and he was a master of public relations. He crafted his own persona and over the course of his lifetime learned how to capitalize on the concept. The Mark Twain Company handled licensing arrangements and endorsements, an original concept at the time. Emerging from this company came such things as patents for Mark Twain Tobacco and Mark Twain Whiskey, creating the earliest forms of a trademark.

While not truly an activist, Twain spoke out against racism and injustice as he witnessed it. The deep anger he felt in such matters was safely channeled through his humorous writings. Twain believed in God while at the same time lambasting churches and the clergy. He invested thousands of dollars in an attempt to become wealthy, and yet he disdained capitalists who preyed upon the underprivileged. Nevertheless, he formed close friendships with the very capitalists he disdained.

Twain maneuvered and bridged social barriers that would have slowed lesser men. He dined with royalty and cooked over a campfire

with rough old miners. He knew the literary elite of B
freely with escaped slaves from the South; he was
traveling around the world as he was in his billiards
During his long stays in Europe he served as Amen   ..cial
diplomat. His friendly, down-home brand of philosophy appealed to all
races and all creeds.

In Mark Twain's lifetime, he was fortunate to have the freedom to
experiment with various types and genres of writing. The enormous
body of work he produced includes travel books, novels, stories, plays,
essays, sketches, poems, and autobiographical writings, not to mention
the personal correspondence and journals kept through the years. The
sheer size of his personal correspondence may never be truly known, but
it's estimated that his 800 surviving pieces fill about 18,000 pages.

In spite of his success, Twain had a few regrets. He did very little
writing while at "home," meaning the United States, claiming a lack of
concentration due to social demands and interruptions. Only later did
he realize he had the power to control this issue. He said, "I wish now
that I had done differently and had persisted in writing when at home. I
could easily have done it, although I thought I could not. I seemed to
think then that I was never going to grow old, but I know better than
that now."

Twain longed to be counted with the literary elite of his day, and
yet he knew he was the voice for the common man. He grew to accept
that as his calling in life. "My books are water," he once said. "Those of
the geniuses are wine. Everybody drinks water."

Mark Twain: "The Lincoln of our Literature"

Among nineteenth-century American writers, Samuel Langhorne Clemens, writing as Mark Twain, created some of the most enduring images of that sense of place, character, and ethos that readers identify as distinctively, even peculiarly, American. From his first published story, "Jim Smiley and His Jumping Frog" (1865) to his last, "The Mysterious Stranger" (published posthumously in 1916), Twain's critical weapon against what he saw as the provincialism and hypocrisy of American life and politics is the humor of a detached observer, a wry and skeptical authorial voice. But we already know about hypocrisy in the everyday workings of the American dream, which is why we have come to call it a dream. Twain shows us something more—an American narrative; fictions of a particular place and time; fictions drawn from indigenous folktale and foundational myth that continue to inform our understanding of the push westward that shaped all of American history to the end of the nineteenth century and the closing of the frontier. Permeating all American narrative, critics such as Toni Morrison and David L. Smith suggest, is the issue of slavery against ideal and real freedom. Twain treats slavery in many of his works with satire and irony, but he finds no imaginative resolution.

The post-Civil War years brought a hunger for culture, and a desire for improvement of all kinds drove American arts and industry. Americans shared an optimism partaking of Constitutional idealism, Emersonian self-reliance, and a Protestant inflected belief in human progress and limitless possibility. Technological innovation inspired imaginations as the completion of a transcontinental railroad closed distances and began to make time a commodity. With middle-class ambition one from even modest beginnings could become, it seemed, anything. The national exuberance that filtered through the inevitable contrast between democratic ideals and everyday realities of class, commerce, delusion, and outright greed provided the perfect foil for the humorist.

In the 1875 version of the "Jumping Frog" story, published in *Mark Twain's Sketches, New and Old*, the contrast in diction between the narrator, an Eastern newspaperman, and the storyteller, Simon Wheeler, plays upon a clash between the language of the established order and a subversive folk-style narrative set on enveloping it—or at least outmaneuvering it.

> [Wheeler,] dozing comfortably by the bar-room stove of the dilapidated tavern in the decayed mining camp of Angel's backed me into a corner and blockaded me there with his chair and then sat down and reeled off the monotonous narrative which follows this paragraph.... [A]ll through the interminable narrative there ran a vein of impressive earnestness and sincerity, which showed me plainly that, so far from his imagining that there was anything ridiculous or funny about his story, he regarded it as a really important matter, and admired its two heroes as men of transcendent genius in *finesse*.

The narrator is immune to the backwoods charms of exaggeration and tall tale. Wheeler, too, seems unaware of the humor of his own tale. Twain's confidence as an artist is evident in the beginning of this tale when the reader is informed that the story to come will be tiresome, yet when the story ends in the company of the irritable and pompous narrator, Wheeler's company is preferred after all. As if comparing the "education" of the jumping frog to the respectable refinements the easterner, Wheeler points out the superior qualities of the frog:

> Smiley said all a frog wanted was education, and he could do 'most anything—and I believe him. Why, I've seen him set

Dan'l Webster down here on this floor—Dan'l Webster was
the name of the frog—and sing out, "Flies, Dan'l, flies!" and
quicker'n you could wink he'd spring straight up and snake a
fly off 'n the counter there, and flop down on the floor ag'in
as solid as a gob of mud, and fall to scratching the side of his
head with his hind foot as indifferent as if he hadn't no idea
he'd been doin' any more'n any frog might do. You never see
a frog so modest and straightfor'ard as he was, for all he was
so gifted.

Wheeler clearly has narrative gifts and a sense of humor that the
newspaperman lacks—and he, like the unknown personage who has sent
this foil to him, seems to know it. In what Twain called a "villainous
backwoods sketch," one reader observed that "all schemes fail, even to
an anticipated crisis and resolution. What stands is the telling of the tale;
what persists is a preposterous reification of *good breeding*. What also
persists is Twain's intuitive interpretation of the American dream of
egalitarianism and opportunity that would so often disappoint him."

The disappearing western frontier had become a treasure of
indigenous narrative of Indians and slaves, tall tales, and myth that
would contribute to a national identity, to an authentic American history
distinct from the European. F. Scott Fitzgerald would write of Twain
and his character Huck Finn, "[He] took the first journey *back*. He was
the first to look *back* at the republic from the perspective of the West.
His eyes were the first eyes that ever looked at us objectively that were
not eyes from overseas." Before shaping Huck Finn's perspective,
however, Twain would rework his letters to the *Daily Alta California* as a
correspondent to Europe and the Holy Land and write *The Innocents
Abroad* (1869). As in "The Jumping Frog," in *Innocents* Twain juxtaposes
the breadth of European art and history with the heretical newness of
American experience come to claim its place in the world—or at least to
assert its occupation of a vast stretch of it and to assert an abrasive
ignorance of any cultural debt to Europe. Weary from "study and
sightseeing," the group of American correspondents enjoys making their
Italian guide "suffer":

Many a man has wished in his heart he could do without
his guide; but knowing he could not, has wished he could get

some amusement out of him as a remuneration for the affliction of his society. We accomplished this latter matter, and if our experience can be made useful to others they are welcome to it.

Guides know about enough English to tangle every thing up so that a man can make neither head or tail of it. They know their story by heart—the history of every statue, painting, cathedral or other wonder they show you. They know it and tell it as a parrot would—and if you interrupt, and throw them off the track, they have to go back and begin over again. All their lives long, they are employed in showing strange things to foreigners and listening to their bursts of admiration. It is what prompts children to say "smart" things, and do absurd ones, and in other ways "show off" when company is present. It is what makes gossips turn out in rain and storm to go and be the first to tell a startling bit of news. Think, then, what a passion it becomes with a guide, whose privilege it is, every day, to show to strangers wonders that throw them into perfect ecstasies of admiration! He gets so that he could not by any possibility live in a soberer atmosphere. After we discovered this, we *never* went into ecstacies any more—we never admired any thing—we never showed any but impassible faces and stupid indifference in the presence of the sublimest wonders a guide had to display. We had found their weak point. We have made good use of it ever since. We have made some of those people savage, at times, but we have never lost our own serenity.

The doctor asks the questions, generally, because he can keep his countenance, and look more like an inspired idiot, and throw more imbecility into the tone of his voice than any man that lives. It comes natural to him.

There is an adolescent quality to the tactics of the "little party" that may bring to mind the very same quality still perceived as characteristically American—an entire nation of "joyous heretics" who may at any time return to the Old World with new and irreverent eyes. "'Our little party' functions throughout *The Innocents Abroad* as a portable audience," Henry B. Wonham notes in *Mark Twain and the Art of the Tall Tale*

(1993), "a traveling yarn-spinning community whose exchange of yarns and interpretations allows Twain to locate his narrator's verbal pranks in a situational context." In the rhetorical manner of the tall tale, Twain dramatizes rather than describes the narrator parodying "his own credulity, which is rooted in an inherited assumption of European superiority in matters of taste and refinement.... Twain's narrator arrives in the Old World with only a yarn spinner's shrewdness to compensate for an abundance of ignorance ... yet he neither apologizes for his rough humor nor makes pretenses toward understanding what is alien to his sensibility."

In *Persona and Humor in Mark Twain's Early Writings* (1995) Don Florence observes that, in *Innocents* "both European and American attitudes appear ridiculous. Twain seems satisfied neither with the fixity and reverence of the Old World nor with the fluidity and irreverence of the New World.... [He] lampoons the European compulsion to preserve the past, but he also implies a touch of contempt for America because of its short memory and ruthless drive toward the future." Romantic illusions, "fostered by innocence or distance, [yield] to disappointment as Twain gains experience or a closer look":

> Seen from the anchorage or from a mile or so up the Bosporus, it is by far the handsomest city we have seen. Its dense array of houses swell upward from the water's edge, and spreads over the domes of many hills; and the gardens that peep out here and there, the great globes of the mosques, and the countless minarets that meet the eye every where, invest the metropolis with the quaint Oriental aspect one dreams of when he reads books of eastern travel. Constantinople makes a noble picture.
>
> But its attractiveness begins and ends with its picturesqueness. From the time one starts ashore till he gets back again, he execrates it. The boat he goes in is admirably miscalculated for the service it is built for.... You start to go to a given point and you run in fifty different directions before you get there....
>
> .... Ashore it was—well, it was an eternal circus. People were thicker than bees in those narrow streets, and the men were dressed in all the outrageous, outlandish, idolatrous,

extravagant, thunder-and-lightning costumes that ever a
tailor with the delirium tremens and seven devils could
conceive of.

Twain's humor, says Florence, is forced here, "admirably miscalculated
to take him anywhere, and he is left rudderless and adrift. Play has
degenerated into confusion; nothing seems true to him. The guidebooks
lie; dreams lie; pictures lie. Dreams and pictures project human wishes,
not reality." Twain's humor pivots upon the contrast between the vulgar
realities of foreign societies and their attractions seemingly out of
context even in their own context. Europe and the Middle East
disappoint him.

The foundation of Twain's humor is always in the social encounter,
the conversation by which both pretensions and sympathies are revealed.
Without the personal encounter, we are all in essence adrift, all
susceptible to some sort of personally shaped delirium tremens. "Every
ship is a romantic object," wrote Emerson in *Experience* (1862), "except
that we sail in. Embark, and the romance quits our vessel, and hangs on
every other sail in the horizon.... The years teach much which the days
never know." Centuries of European history set against the newness of
American experience could provoke a sort of mass hallucination, Twain
suggests, as in "The Petrified Man (1862)," a satire on the news
proclaiming the discovery of the Cardiff Man near Syracuse, New York,
something believed authentic was unearthed.

In "The Petrified Man," published in the Virginia City *Territorial
Enterprise*, Twain had already set forth the comic sense that would thread
through *The Innocents Abroad*. An article about the discovery of a
mummified man with fingers making a rude gesture, Twain thought the
story as an obvious and very funny joke, but a gullible public took it as
fact. More interestingly, the stone man is worthless as art and has
nothing to do with antiquity, but it brings the idea of history and the
nurturing of national myths into play. "With a bit of instant aging," critic
Tom Quirk points out in *Mark Twain: A Study of the Short Fiction* (1997),
"a change of name, and the consensus approval or art critics, it suddenly
becomes a revered masterpiece.... [Twain's] defense (and censure) of the
living present over and against the dead hand of the past contributed to
an articulation of essentially American and democratic values."

Twain's European tour, like the excavation of mummies, reflects
the Emersonian observation that "All inquiry into antiquity ... is the

desire to do away [with] this wild, savage and preposterous There or Then, and introduce in its place the Here and the Now (*History* 1847)." Twain set an American vernacular and spirit of place against an established and still formidable cultural order. He accomplishes this more elaborately in *Roughing It* (1872): Twain's memories of his overland trip to Nevada in 1861 and elements of the tall tale structure the conversation between a reasonable narrator and Bemis, a fellow traveler who is chased up a tree by a wounded buffalo. Twain juxtaposes elements that evoke the dignified tradition of an English fox hunt with comic pretensions on the American frontier:

> Next morning just before dawn, when about five hundred and fifty miles from St Joseph, our mud-wagon broke down. We were to be delayed five or six hours, and therefore we took horses, by invitation, and joined a party who were just starting on a buffalo hunt. It was noble sport galloping over the plain in the dewy freshness of the morning, but our part of the hunt ended in disaster and disgrace, for a wounded buffalo bull chased the passenger Bemis nearly two miles, and then he forsook his horse and took to a lone tree. He was very sullen about the matter for some twenty-four hours, but at last he began to often little by little ....

The American vernacular and the satirical mirroring of English tradition work in both directions: The fox hunt is ridiculous, and the buffalo hunt no less so.

Tom Sawyer (1876) was Twain's first novel. Though the earlier *The Gilded Age* (1873), co-written with Charles Dudley Warner, is also called a novel, its conventional treatment of plot and character fails to fulfill what Twain accomplished in *Tom Sawyer*: the consistent and sustained development of a central character in relationship with other characters with defined personal and social circumstances set in a specific time and place. As much as its setting on the frontier, the language of the novel, the American idiom, separates *Tom* Sawyer from the British tradition.

Stuart Hutchinson, in *Mark Twain—Humour on the Run*, reminds us that the use of an American vernacular was "a crucial issue" for nineteenth century American writers: "With emerging American language to draw on, they had resources unknown to their British counterparts. They had resistances to their inheritance of British literature. [British] plots, as Tom Sawyer was to discover, did not always work on the banks of the Mississippi (p 12)."

William Dean Howells, Twain's lifelong friend and editor of the *Atlantic Monthly*, reviewed *Tom Sawyer* in May 1876:

> Mr. Clemens ... has taken the boy of the Southwest for the hero of his new book and has presented him with a fidelity to circumstance which loses no charm by being realistic in the highest degree, and which gives incomparably the best picture of life in that region as yet known to fiction. The town where Tom Sawyer was born and brought up is some such idle, shabby little Mississippi River town as Mr. Clemens has so well described in his piloting reminiscences, but Tom belongs to the better sort of people in it, and has been bred to fear God and dread the Sunday-school according to the strictest rights of faiths that have characterised all the respectability of the West. His subjection in these respects does not so deeply affect his inherent tendencies but that he makes himself a beloved burden to the poor, tender-hearted old aunt who brings him up with his orphan brother and sister, and struggles vainly with his manifold sins, actual and imaginary ....
>
> The tale is dramatically wrought, and the subordinate characters are treated with the same graphic force that sets Tom alive before us.... Many village people and local notables are introduced in well-concealed character; the whole little town lives in the reader's sense, with its religiousness, its lawlessness, its droll social distinctions, its civilisation qualified by slaveholding, and its traditions of the wilder West which has passed away.

Howells' kind review mentions but does not probe aspects of the novel that later critics would less benignly examine, such as the Calvinist religious sensibility that informs the "respectability of the West," and the slaveholding that has in large part built this new civilization. Of the humor in *Tom Sawyer*, Hutchinson finds an echo of Clemens' despair over the accompanying failure of humor to set things right in the world that Florence observed of *The Innocents Abroad*: "Might we conclude that [Twain's humor] is American in the sense that it functions entirely on behalf of itself and is never in aid of anything, so that Twain would eventually face despair when the jokes no longer provided relief (p 15)?" Perhaps Clemens would despair, but the task of the writerly persona, Mark Twain, is to keep despair at bay with all the resources of fiction.

Tom Sawyer is not a tall tale, nor is it a sequential travelogue. Twain's novel relies on a consistent verisimilitude that critic Bernard DeVoto, in *Mark Twain at Work* (1942) nonetheless finds wanting:

> [*Tom Sawyer*] is more profoundly true to the phantasies of boyhood than any other ever written, and the maturity's nostalgia for what it once was, though it has forged the symbols that seem likely to express boyhood more permanently than any other in literature, it cannot be thought of as comprehensive or profound realism. The term is dangerous; certainly the forged symbol transcends literalism and the truth of *Tom Sawyer* is the kind of truth that only symbols can express—like the symbols of *Antigone* or *Macbeth*. But you need only differentiate boyhood from its symbols to perceive how much of it Mark ignores. There is, we have seen no sex—none of the curiosity, the shame, the torment, the compulsion of young ignorance groping in mystery. Becky and Tom in the empty schoolroom do not belong in the same world with any pair of ten-year-olds in a hayloft, and though Tom thinking of her by the dark river is profoundly true he never goes on to think of her as any boy must in the years when girls are last known to be females....
>
> Furthermore, Tom's immortal daydreams never get much above the childish level ... [W]as there no glace forward as well, had he no nebulous, inarticulate vision of growing up, did he get no nearer than this to the threshold of ambition and desire, where boyhood darkly flowers in frustrated poetry? ... Is a boy's mind no wider and no deeper than Tom's? Where are the brutalities, the sternnesses, the strengths, the perceptions, and the failures that will eventually make a man; Well, in part Mark's will was to ignore such things, ... [a]nd in part he was incapable of the

analysis which the probing of motives and psychological intricacies requires; his understanding was intuitive and concrete and he was sure only of behaviour, fumbling when he had to be introspective.

The "phantasies of boyhood" are not real; in that which evokes the phantasies may reside whatever may be thought "real," but Twain never touches upon such boyhood secrets. Of course, Twain's failure to deal with the symbols of awakening sexuality cannot be blamed solely upon his failure to face them. Had Twain depicted the sexual tensions of ten-year-olds *Tom Sawyer* would not have been published. That aside, DeVoto's most cogent point is that Tom has no interior life. But Tom does possess a most Emersonian quality of self-reliance as a boy (as would Huck Finn) who is "independent, irresponsible, ... [trying and sentencing people] on their merits, in the swift, summary way of boys, as good, bad, interesting, silly, eloquent, troublesome...." Tom "cumbers himself never about consequences, about interests" but always "gives a genuine verdict (*Self-Reliance*,1847)." He may be authentic, but he is limited to a prepubescent boy's emotional existence.

Freudian psychoanalysis, either as science or literary criticism, was not yet on the horizon for Emerson before the Civil War, nor did it inform the rigid religious and civic precepts that characterized the American West of Twain's time in the last half of the century. Tom Sawyer is a nostalgic symbol, a boy who seems to have no future as an adult (Critics have pointed out the contrast between this aspect of *Tom Sawyer* and Stephen Crane's *The Red Badge of Courage* (1895), a psychological study of a young man, Henry Fleming, and his nightmarish progress toward manhood in battle during the Civil War.) But DeVoto argues in its favor that *Tom Sawyer* ... perfectly preserves something of the American experience, more of American dreaming, and still more of the beauty that was our heritage and that still conditions both our national memory and our phantasy.... Time has stopped short; the frontier has passed by and the industrial revolution is not yet born. Life is confident and untroubled, moves serenely at an unhurried pace, fulfills itself in peace. Islanded in security, in natural beauty, St. Petersburg is an idyll of what we once were, of what it is now more than ever necessary to remember we once were. Here also the book captures and will keep secure forever a part of America—of America over the hills and far away.

In this vision of a mythical America, problematic even when DeVoto's book was published in 1942, racism and the fear of the outsider, carried through the novel by the outcast and outlaw Injun Joe, remain embedded and unexamined in the novel. Injun Joe's horrible intentions toward a woman and his death by starvation stand in contrast to the sweetness of the schoolroom encounter between Tom and Becky. James Cox, in "Remarks on the Sad Initiation of Huckleberry Finn" (*Sewanee Review*, July-September 1954), examines the contribution of Injun Joe to the structure of the *Tom Sawyer*:

> The violence and terror which are just beneath the surface of the boys' world regularly erupt into it. After the pleasures of the schoolroom comes the dark and unknown night, bringing with it fear and death.... Tom's repeated death fantasies ... give [his] character depth and complexity. Time after time the rhythm of the novel is expressed in terms of his death wish. Tom retires into solitude envisioning the mourning of the village when its inhabitants realize that he is no more. The culmination of the Jackson Island episode is the triumphal return of Tom and his two cronies to witness their own funerals. Even when death closes in on Tom and Becky in the darkness of the cave, Tom awaits it with a certain pleasure.
>
> But there is another death, a death brutal and ghastly, lurking just beyond the boys' world and constantly impinging on it; it is the death in the graveyard and the death of Injun Joe—instead of warmth and protection this death is informed with terror. To see it as a brutal fact waiting in the adult world is to look with wistful eyes at that other death. The cave episode, fantastic from a "realistic" point of view, is oddly appropriate because it embodies the paradox of death and isolation; it is in the cave that Tom, in the very arms of the warm shadow, manages to find the will to force his way to light and safety; but it is also in the cave that Injun Joe meets one of the most violent and horrifying deaths in our literature. The two images of death are united in the cave, and it is hardly pure coincidence that Injun Joe, the demon who has haunted Tom's dreams, lies dead at the sealed

doorway of the abyss from which Tom has escaped.... [H]e
has glimpsed the sheer terror at the centre of his childhood
image of death. His immediate return to the cave to seize the
treasure suggests his inner triumph.

The discovery of the treasure, significantly hidden under Injun
Joe's cross, enables Tom to enter heroically the ranks of the respectable.
Of course, he has been slyly respectable all along. Even when he breaks
the law he does so with the intimate knowledge that he is expected to
break it. His acute dramatic sense enables him to see the part he is to
play, and he is therefore constantly aware of his participation in sacred
social rites. This awareness results in a kind of compulsive badness in his
nature.... As the curtain drops there is triumphant confirmation of Tom's
membership in the cult of the respectable. He is even trying to sell the
club to Huck, cautioning him to remain a member of society because if
one is to belong to Tom Sawyer's Outlaw Gang one must, paradoxically,
obey the law.

Injun Joe's brutality and the horror of his death embody fears that
must be kept in the subconscious if one is to live in the world. As a
symbol, Injun Joe carries the distinction that Tom consistently makes
between religious superstition (Injun Joe's cross) and what he deems
most truly sacred (social rites). Hutchinson remarks that Joe may
embody Twain's subconsciousness: "Injun Joe might be the author's
violent rage with all the complacency he is apparently settling for in *Tom
Sawyer*."

Arthur G. Pettit, in "Mark Twain's Attitude Toward the Negro in
the West," (*The Western Historical Quarterly*, January 1970), remarks
upon Twain's racism and how it is woven into his work. Pettit is clearly
unimpressed with Twain's movement away from racist thinking:

... Clemens decisively switched his political allegiance from
the South to the North early in the Western period, [but] his
attitude toward the Negro remained essentially the same,
precisely because, unlike some of his other southern traits,
his Negrophobia coincided with, rather than deviated from,
the Western norm. Fleeing from a terrible war, and not very
interested in the survival of the Union beyond whatever
impact that survival might have on his own existence,

Clemens found the Far West an ideal temporary society, and a most congenial environment in which to practice his first extensive experiments with the Negro as the comic butt, the minstrel stooge, the inane, foolish "yassah" man of long-standing minstrel tradition.

Although Mark Twain would continue to explore this tradition of the black buffoon as scapegoat for white humor long after his experience in the West was over, Samuel Clemens reached the peak of his race prejudice during the Western years. Soon after his arrival in the East in 1867, as a potential member of the eastern establishment, as well as the son-in-law of a man who had been a leading conductor on the New York underground railway before the war and a public man of letters under pressure to re-evaluate some of his more extreme feelings about the Negro, Clemens in fact did begin to shift his emotional allegiance (the kind he valued most) to a partly reconstructed view of the black man. In this sense, then, the half-decade that Clemens spent in the Far West serves as a watershed period in his reaction to the Negro—a turning point that, within a year after his return to the East, would lead him to launch a new career of at least liberal lip service to the black race.

Twain was most certainly influenced by the abolitionist activities of his in-laws, the Langdon family. Pettit points out that when Livy Langdon's father asked for letters of reference, Clemens sought them only from his Unionist and Republican friends in the West. Pettit continues, in "Mark Twain and the Negro" (*Journal of Negro History*, April 1971):

> Yet it would be hazardous to suggest that Clemens's somewhat altered attitudes toward Black men were grounded entirely on public expedience rather than private conviction. On the contrary, his exposure to men of wider intellectual horizons in Europe the Middle East, and the Eastern states made it inevitable that he would revise some of his more outspoken racist views. The vacillatory, faltering, and incomplete nature of his reconstruction regarding the

Negro during this period simply underscores the difficulty of such a conversion, not that a partial conversion was not taking place.

Still groping, still adjusting to the society in which he had voluntarily encased himself, it is not surprising that Mark Twain's ability to render effective Black character portrayals still lagged somewhat behind Clemens's personal efforts to acquire a more tolerant attitude toward Negroes in general. That he failed to go even farther during this period probably speaks at least as much for the society and times in which he lived as for Clemens himself.

Hutchinson responds:

> *Tom Sawyer* may confirm Pettit's point about the difficulty even an enlightened Twain had in creating "effective Black characters"... [but] *Tom Sawyer* was never imagined as a powerful enough vehicle to carry the most divisive issue of Twain's personal life, and of the life of his nation. Nonetheless, the novel has a representative of another race to which enormous injustice has been done. Even in this nostalgic book, Twain engages with the complicating energies of his culture. Fantasies of the outcast indulged in Tom meet their desperate counterpart in the Ishmaelite Injun Joe, the son of mixed race and visible evidence of those acts of depredation against the Native American by which white society had established itself.

That Injun Joe is of mixed race is a sign of both his racial degradation and his kinship with a white society. Cynthia Griffin Wolff, in *"The Adventures of Tom Sawyer*: A Nightmare Vision of American Boyhood" (*The Massachusetts Review*, Winter 1980), makes the connection between the fantasy violence of Tom's rebellion against the constraints imposed upon him by Aunt Polly and other figures of authority and the violence of the outlaw Injun Joe:

> Given the precarious balancing of control and violence in Tom's fantasies, we can easily comprehend his terrified

fascination with Injun Joe's incursions into the "safety" of St Petersburg. Accidentally witness to Injun Joe's murderous attack, Tom's first response is characteristic: he writes an oath in blood, pledging secrecy "Huck Finn and Tom Sawyer swears they will keep mum about this and they wish they may Drop down dead in Their tracks if they ever tell and Rot." It is an essentially "literary" maneuver, and Tom's superstitious faith in its efficacy is of a piece with the "rules" he has conned from books about outlaws. However, Injun Joe cannot easily be relegated to the realm of such villains. It is as if one element in Tom's fantasy world has torn loose and broken away from him, roaming restlessly—a ruthless predator—genuinely and mortally dangerous.

He has murdered a man, but perversely, he does not flee. Instead, he loiters about the town in disguise, waiting for the moment to arrive when he can take "revenge." Humiliated once by the Widow Douglas's husband (no longer available to the Indian's rage), Joe plans to work his will upon the surviving mate. "Oh, don't kill her! Don't do that!" his nameless companion implores.

"Kill? Who said anything about killing? I would kill *him* if he was here; but not her. When you want to get revenge on a woman you don't kill her—bosh! you go for her looks. You slit her nostrils—you notch her ears like a sow!

I'll tie her to the bed. If she bleeds to death, is that my fault? I'll not cry, if she does."

It is almost a parody of Tom's concocted "rules" for outlaws; even Injun Joe flinches from killing a woman. Sadistic torture (of a clearly sexual nature) is sufficient.

His grievance is twofold against the absence of the man who would be his natural antagonist; and then against the woman who has inherited the man's property and authority. Seen in this light, his condition is not unlike the hero's. Tom, denied the example of mature men whom he might emulate, is left with no model to define an adult nature of his own. Tom, adrift in the matriarchal world—paying the continuous "punishment" of guilt for the "crime" of his resentment at genteel restraints, conceiving carefully measured fantasies within which to voice (and mime) his feelings. Injun Joe is Tom's shadow self, a potential for retrogression and destructiveness that cannot be permitted abroad.

Yet the genuine vanquishment is no easy task. No other adult male plays so dominant a role in the novel as Injun Joe. Indeed, no other male's name save Huck's and Tom's is uttered so often.... The Indian, an outcast and a savage, is unpredictable; he may turn fury upon the villagers or act as ultimate executioner for Tom. When Tom's tentative literary gestures prove insufficient, desperate remedies are necessary: Twain invoked the ultimate adventure. Death.

Death as the "ultimate adventure" may also be seen as the ultimate freedom, but surely not for Tom. The conventional moral scheme of *Tom Sawyer* ensures the containment of Injun Joe's violence. This moral scheme is disrupted in *Huckleberry Finn* as Huck is driven into flight by problems that have no resolution, only to encounter more of the same.

Tom Sawyer anticipates F. Scott Fitzgerald's Jay Gatsby. Gatsby will recall Daisy with the longing found in Tom's daydreams of Becky Thatcher, dreams which gave Tom "such an agony of pleasurable suffering that he worked it over and over again in his mind and set it up in new and varied lights, till he wore it threadbare. At last he rose up sighing and departed in the darkness." Critics seem in agreement that Tom and Becky as adults would be a most conventional couple. With the assistance of Judge Thatcher, Tom is assured of a prosperous and respectable place in the community. But, Hutchinson observes, "[s]ince Tom will never grow up, ... Tom thus matches Gatsby, who is himself killed before reaching fulfilment. The rewards and accommodation beckoning the hero will never be attained. Dispossession prevails, at least by implication...."

Tom will be dispossessed; Injun Joe is already dispossessed. The unsettled and unsettling emotional kinship between them provides the most powerful and tension in the novel. In *The Adventures of Huckleberry Finn* (1884, London; 1885, America) Twain offers a more complex—and more controversial—portrayal of post-Civil War regional character and experience on the Mississippi River.

The Adventures of Huckleberry Finn was from its publication a very popular book—except in Massachusetts where, in March 1885, it was banned by the Concord Free Public Library, which famously pronounced it "more suited to the slums than to intelligent, respectable people." The ban provoked widespread response and probably helped to sell more copies than the most ambitious of advertising campaigns. Victor Fisher, in "Huck Finn Reviewed: The Reception of *Huckleberry Finn* in the United States, 1885-97" (*American Literary Realism: 1870-1910*, Spring 1983), concludes that:

> Despite the evident distaste in some quarters for Mark Twain's commercial success, and despite his failure to secure an early favorable review "by an authority," *Huck Finn* was reviewed favorably and intelligently in a number of newspapers—in particular, the New York *Sun*, the Hartford *Courant*, *Post*, and *Times*, and the San Francisco *Chronicle*. It was also well defended by these and others in the discussion of the Concord Library ban. Within six years of publication, *Huck Finn* had left most of its detractors behind. In 1891, the year that the Webster company [founded by Twain in 1884] published the second edition, Andrew Lang [in the *London Illustrated New*, February 14, 1891] pronounced it "nothing less" than a "masterpiece."

Punch magazine (January 4, 1896) called it a "Homeric book;" and *Harper's Monthly* (September 1896) advertised the book as already part of the chronicle of American history: "After the humor of the book has had its way then the pathos will become apparent, and later still will come the recognition of the value of these sketches as pictures of a civilization now ended."

Not only critics, but creative writers weighed in heavily on *Huckleberry Finn*. T.S. Eliot, in his preface to the 1950 edition of the novel remarks that *Tom Sawyer* had not prepared him for the literary significance of Twain's masterpiece. Eliot's comparison of the two novels measures Twain's literary achievement in *Huckleberry Finn*:

> We look at Tom as the smiling adult does: Huck we do not look at—we see the world through his eyes. The two boys

are not merely different types; they were brought into existence by different processes.

Tom Sawyer is an orphan. But he has his aunt; he has, as we learn later, other relatives; and he has the environment into which he fits. He is wholly a social being. When there is a secret band to be formed, it is Tom who organizes it and prescribes the rules. Huck Finn is alone: there is no more solitary character in fiction. The fact that he has a father only emphasises his loneliness; and he views his father with a terrifying detachment. So we come to see Huck himself in the end as one of the permanent symbolic figures of fiction; not unworthy to take a place with Ulysses, Faust, Don Quixote, Don Juan, Hamlet and other great discoveries that man has made about himself.

It would seem that Mark Twain was a man who—perhaps like most of us—never became in all respects mature. We might even say that the adult side of him was boyish, and that only the boy in him, that was Huck Finn, was adult. As Tom Sawyer grown up, he wanted success and applause (Tom himself always needs an audience). He wanted prosperity, a happy domestic life of a conventional kind, universal approval, and fame. All of these things he obtained. As Huck Finn he was indifferent to all these things; and being composite of the two, Mark Twain both strove for them, and resented their violation of his integrity. Hence he became the humorist and even clown: with his gifts, a certain way to success, for everyone could enjoy his writings without the slightest feeling of discomfort, self-consciousness or self-criticism. And hence, on the other hand, his pessimism and misanthropy. To be a misanthrope is to be in some way divided; or it is a sign of an uneasy conscience.

Huck Finn is a character who transcends his circumstances in ways that Twain could not. Eliot's perceives the split in Twain's personality that Twain could nonetheless explore—but never reconcile—in his treatments of Tom and Huck. We may think of Huck as one of "the great discoveries that man has made about himself" and at the same time wonder why such self-discovery was not more therapeutic for the author.

At the end of Chapter 18 and the beginning of Chapter 19, Twain seems to romanticize the free-moving life on a raft or, perhaps, an openness to nature and unknown possibilities. But the king and the duke disrupt the idyll, moving Huck to draw a significant conclusion about how to get along in civilization, and confirmation of what he'd learned from his father: "It didn't take me long to make up my mind that these liars warn't no kings nor dukes, at all, just low-down humbugs and frauds.... If I never learnt nothing else out of pap, I learnt that the best way to get along with his kind of people is to let them have their own way." The king and the duke, says Hutchinson, return Huck and Jim "to corrupted identities which will always shape their lives (p 71)." Evocative of the Romantic idea of the uncorrupted child in harmony with nature, Twain's Huck will never be in harmony with anything. But, Eliot continues, "It is Huck who gives the book style. The River gives the book its form. But for the River, the book might be only a sequence of adventures with a happy ending. A river ... is the only natural force that can wholly determine the course of human peregrination.... It is a treacherous and capricious dictator." The Mississippi River is notorious for its shifting banks and perilous sandbars. As a symbol and as a force greater than human, Eliot unveils a significant part of Twain's psyche as he probes Huck's character in relationship to the river:

> [T]he River God is [Twain's] God. It is as a native that he accepts the River God, and it is the subjection of Man that gives to Man his dignity. For without some kind of God, Man is not even very interesting....
>
> For Huckleberry Finn, neither a tragic nor a happy ending would be suitable. No worldly success or social satisfaction, no domestic consummation would be worthy of him; a tragic end also would reduce him to the level of those whom we pity. Huck Finn must come from nowhere and be bound for nowhere.... His existence questions the values of America as much as the values of Europe; he is as much an affront to the "pioneer spirit" as he is to "business enterprise"; he is in a state of nature as detached as the state of the saint.... He belongs neither to the Sunday School nor to the Reformatory. He has no beginning or end. Hence, he can only disappear; and his disappearance can only be

accomplished by bringing forward another performer [Tom
Sawyer] to obscure the disappearance in a cloud of
whimsicalities.

Like Huckleberry Finn, the River itself has no beginning
or end. In its beginning, it is not yet the River; in its end, it
is no longer the River.

The appearance—or, as some have called it, the intrusion—of Tom
Sawyer into the novel at the end would seem to support the idea that
Twain, like all writers of fiction, reveals much about himself in his work.
Huck, who belongs to no place, time, or relationship, is masked by Tom,
the performer/writer/lecturer who never matures. The present, with its
contradictions and ironies, is inescapable.

Booker T. Washington, in the *North American Review* (June 1910),
in the year of Twain's death, composed the first response by a black critic
to *Huckleberry Finn*:

> "I do not believe any one can read this story closely," he
> wrote, "without becoming aware of the deep sympathy of the
> author in 'Jim'.... [O]ne cannot fail to observe that in some
> way or other the author without making any comment and
> without going out of his way, has somehow succeeded in
> making his readers feel a genuine respect for 'Jim,' in spite of
> the ignorance he displays. I cannot help feeling that in this
> character Mark Twain has, perhaps, exhibited his sympathy
> and interest in the masses of the negro people.

At the time, Jim Crow laws, thousands of lynchings, and the
disenfranchisement of blacks in most southern states make Washington's
response to the novel puzzling to later critics. Toni Morrison, in *Playing
in the Dark: Whiteness and the Literary Imagination* (1992), considers the
dual agenda of the presumed white reader and the mechanisms of racial
oppression at work in the novel. Her reading of the novel places Jim at
its core, giving *Huckleberry Finn* its structure and transcendent meaning:

> On this young but street-smart innocent, Huck, who is
> virginally uncorrupted by bourgeois yearnings, fury, and
> helplessness, Mark Twain inscribes a critique of slavery and

the pretensions of the would-be middle class, a resistance to the loss of Eden and the difficulty of becoming a social individual. The agency, however, for Huck's struggles is the nigger Jim ....

The critical controversy has focused on the collapse of the so-called fatal ending of the novel. It has been suggested that the ending is a brilliant finesse that returns Tom Sawyer to the centre stage where he should be. Or it is a brilliant play on the dangers and limitations of romance. Or it is a sad and confused ending to the book of an author who, after a long blocked period, lost narrative direction; who changed the serious adult focus back to a child's story out of disgust. Or the ending is a valuable learning experience for Jim and Huck for which we and they should be grateful. What is not stressed is that there is no way, given the confines of the novel, for Huck to mature into a moral human being in America without Jim. To let Jim go free, to let him enter the mouth of the Ohio River and pass into free territory, would be to abandon the whole premise of the book. Neither Huck nor Mark Twain can tolerate, in imaginative terms, Jim freed. That would blast the predilection from its mooring.

Thus the fatal ending becomes the elaborate deferment of a necessary and necessarily unfree Africanist character's escape, because freedom has no meaning to Huck or to the text without the spectre of enslavement, the anodyne to individualism; the yardstick of absolute power over the life of another; the signed, marked, informing, and mutating presence of a black slave.

The novel addresses at every point in its structural edifice, and lingers over in every fissure, the slave's body and personality: the way it speaks, what passion legal or illicit it is prey to, what pain it can endure, what limits, if any, there are to its suffering, what possibilities there are for forgiveness, compassion, love. Two things strike us in this novel: the apparently limitless store of love and compassion the black man has for his white friend and white masters; and his assumption that the whites are indeed what they say they

are, superior, and adult.... It is not what Jim seems that
warrants inquiry, but what Mark Twain, Huck, and especially
Tom need from him that should solicit our attention. In that
sense the book may indeed be "great" because in its
structure, in the hell it puts its readers through at the end, the
frontal debate it forces, it simulates and describes the
parasitical nature of white freedom.

Morrison argues persuasively that Twain could move Jim neither away
from slavery—although he could imagine him a runaway, the possibility
of freedom ever deferred—nor into moral adulthood, but *Huckleberry
Finn* would have no importance without him. Traveling the Mississippi
with Huck and Tom would have given us much of the social and
picturesque we already find in the novel, but if we allow Morrison's
reading to guide us, the very idea of freedom that launches their
adventure has little moral weight when nothing is at stake, least of all
their freedom to travel the river as they wish. For Jim, everything is at
stake and, whether or not we are convinced of "the parasitical nature of
white freedom," Jim is the character who requires a destination, a
resolution, and Huck's struggle is chained to his. But Twain deflects this
agenda, claiming that *Huckleberry Finn* is essentially "a book of mine
where a sound heart and a deformed conscience come into collision and
conscience suffers defeat ... [Huck] does right, but cannot think right. At
these junctures his condition is the reverse of what is normally human."
This helps very little in the understanding of the novel unless the reader
sees Jim as a character in his own right, as does Arlin Turner's analysis of
the character of Jim in "Mark Twain and the South: An Affair of Love
and Anger" (*The Southern Review*, April 1968):

> In spite of Jim's presence ... and the danger that he may be
> returned to his owner, slavery is seen only obliquely; not
> slavery but slave doctrine is presented.... [Twain's] main
> concern is not to reveal or even to suggest the plight of the
> slaves: it is rather to expose the folly and the dishonesty
> underlying the prevailing doctrines on race. In this regard
> the book has few equals....
> *Huckleberry Finn* paints the world of the lower Mississippi
> as the whites see it. To be sure, Huck's level of social vision is

little above Jim's, but his sympathy for Jim is inconstant and may seem to imply an identification which does not exist. The white man's doctrine of race superiority is held up to ridicule, but the victim of that doctrine remains unrealized.

Simply put, Twain as a conflicted man and novelist of his time could not imagine and write a slave as a fully developed character. But *Huckleberry Finn* is the strongest anti-racist novel in American or European literature of the period. Jim is not a fully realized character, but his presence is essential, as Morrison points out, to Huck's development as a moral *American*.

Though racism is a pivotal force in the novel, other issues of human conflict erupt in *Huckleberry Finn* alongside it. Huck's reminiscence of his father shapes a terrifying domestic reality of alcohol and rage:

> By-and-by he rolled out and jumped on his feet looking wild and he sees me and went for me. He chased me round and round the place with a clasp-knife, calling me the Angel of Death and saying he would kill me and then I couldn't come for him no more. (Ch 6)

The chase and the threat evoke the grander mythic theme of father resisting death and the ascendancy of the son. Ironically, the contest only seems to drive Huck further into solitude and the determination to form no emotional attachments. But Huck's attachment to his father will never be completely broken. Jim understands this and does not tell Huck of pap's death until he is compelled to do so. James M. Cox, in *Mark Twain: The Fate of Humor* (1966), comments upon Huck's escape from his father by faking his own death:

> This fake murder is probably the most vital and crucial incident of the entire novel. Having killed himself, Huck is "dead" throughout the entire journey down the river. He is indeed the man without identity who is reborn at almost every river bend, not because he desires a new role, but because he must re-create himself to elude the forces which close in on him from every side. The rebirth theme becomes the driving idea behind the entire action.

Coupled with and inseparable from the theme of rebirth is the central image of death. Huck has hardly assumed the role of outcast when he meets Jim, who is also in frantic flight (Interestingly, Jim is considered in terms of property too; his motive for escaping was fear of being sold down the river for $800.), and the two fugitives watch the house of death float by on the swollen Mississippi. When Jim carefully covers up the face of the dead man in the house, the second major image of the novel is forged. These two images, rebirth and death, provide a frame for all succeeding episodes of the arduous initiation. As Huck and Jim move down the river an oncoming steamboat crashes into their raft, forcing the two outcasts to swim for their lives, From this baptism Huck emerges to enter the new life at the Grangerfords under the name of George Jackson. His final act in that life is to cover the dead face of Buck Grangerford, much as Jim had covered Pap's face in the house of death. When the Duke and King come aboard, their unscrupulous schemes force Huck and Jim to appear in new disguises; but the image of death is never absent. It confronts Huck in the little "one-horse town" in Arkansas where Colonel Sherburn shoots the drunken Boggs in cold blood. When the townspeople lift Boggs from the street and take him to the little drug store, Huck peers in through the window to watch him die. The Peter Wilkes episode involves the same central images ... as the Duke and the King force Huck to play the role of an English valet. The final scene of the episode takes place in the graveyard where the mob of townsmen has gathered to exhume the buried Wilkes in an effort to discover whether the Duke and King are imposters. A flash of lightning reveals the dead man with the gold on his breast where Huck had hidden it. The man who has Huck in charge forgets his prisoner in his zeal to see corpse and gold; Huck takes full advantage of the moment and runs out of that world forever.

Finally, the initiation is completed at the Phelps farm. Huck is reborn as Tom Sawyer and this time no image of death appears.... Jim is imprisoned in a cabin much like the one in which Pap locked Huck; Tom Sawyer himself comes to the rescue in the role of Sid Sawyer: the entire household, though not the same as when the novel began, is related to it through strong blood ties. The full import of this initiation becomes more evident when the differences between Huck and Tom Sawyer are examined.

Compared to Huck, Tom Sawyer is a shallow emotional being. Huck is always Pap's son, which, Cox says, "implies his connection with violence and terror," but it also "puts him in touch with the deeper human forces ... which, though they do not enable him to get ahead in an acquisitive society, give him a depth and a reality which far surpass anything Tom Sawyer has dreamed of." Yet the ending of the novel is bitter, confirming that there is no place in civilized society for the likes of Huck Finn, and confirming Twain's own disillusionment:

[A]t the very end of the novel [Huck] immediately feels the compulsion to "light out for the territory" because he knows that to be Huck Finn is to be the outcast beyond the paling fences.... In Tom Sawyer's triumph the hard core of Mark Twain's later disillusion and pessimism is already evident ... [T]he whole outline of the frontier is receding westward before the surge of a small town culture, and it is indeed doomed country into which Huck must retreat.

And Jim is left as the "new American protagonist," Cox intriguingly argues, "that great residue of primitive, fertile force turned free at the end of the novel at the very moment Huck is captured." Twain would return to the problem of slavery in *Pudd'nhead Wilson* (1894).

A year after the publication of *Huckleberry Finn* Twain began his next novel, *A Connecticut Yankee in King Arthur's Court*. The opinion widely held among critics is that *Connecticut Yankee* is a "confused and confusing" work, freighted with Twain's own unresolved inner conflicts. The 1880's and 1890's were a time when one might gain a fortune by investing in new inventions, an idea that intrigued Twain as much as any writerly pursuit. Twain wrote in 1870, "An inventor is a poet—a true poet—and nothing in any degree less than a high order of poet." With the machine, anything was possible. His passionate but failed investment in the Paige typesetting machine left him with a growing pessimism. He began to develop what he would later call his "dream theory," insisting that an "actuality," a reality, was a component of every dream. The fantasies in *Tom Sawyer* and *Huckleberry Finn* had been crucial to the action and mental movements of his characters.

By the mid-1880's, as James L. Johnson writes in *Mark Twain and the Limits of Power*, "He was more and more seriously drawing together ... the Me and the Not Me in a way that would fuse them and make them divinely, or perhaps diabolically, interdependent." In *Connecticut Yankee* Twain employs a dream motif in which Arthurian England "comes to resemble, in its cultural premises and institutions, the actual world of the nineteenth century. The ambiguity is heightened again when, at the end of the tale, Hank believes the nineteenth century to be a dream and the Arthurian world to be real. Twain never resolves the ambiguity." Hank Morgan, a mechanic, is a confident man, sure of his modern abilities to control and shape the world around him to suit his needs—a self-made man:

> I am a Yankee of the Yankees.... Why, I could make anything a body wanted—anything in the world, it didn't make any difference what; and if there wasn't any quick new-fangled way to make a thing, I could invent one—and do it as easy as rolling off a log.

He wakes from the blow to his head into Arthur's Camelot, a world of violence and superstition where, Johnson observes

> [he] will set himself in opposition to all creeds, all history and time. He will become determined that the cultural progress of England should be the lengthened shadow not of tradition but of himself. He would swallow up the men and temples of Arthurian England and refashion them to mirror his own lineaments—efficient, mechanical, and democratic.

Hank will become more humble over the course of the novel, but his egotism does not prevent him from seeing Camelot as it is. He threatens Arthur in a way that, Johnson points out, "reflects through its vocabulary of violence the grim capabilities of an Injun Joe" but with Tom Sawyer's egotism:

> I will smother the whole world in the dead blackness of midnight; I will blot out the sun, and he shall never shine again; the fruits of the earth shall rot for lack of light and warmth, and the peoples of the earth shall famish and die, to the last man.

The eclipse will firmly establish his power and he is "as happy a man as there was in the world ... impatient for to-morrow to come ... [when he would be] the centre of all the nation's wonder and reverence.

"Besides," he muses, "in a business way it would be the making of me; I knew that." Ultimately, the monarchy is restored as Merlin sends Hank not into death but into sleep: "He sleepeth now—and shall sleep thirteen centuries." "Is sleep a punishment?" Johnson asks, "Or a reward?"

> Twain takes Hank Morgan to the verge of destroying civilized objectivity, and even civilization itself. He leads him to the brink of creative madness, but then draws back, appalled at but mesmerized by what he sees there. Finally, he brings Hank Morgan back, to meet—who else?—Mark Twain, a tourist in history and time, and a man strongly susceptible to the spell of Hank's narrative. As Hank falls asleep, Twain takes up the manuscript and drifts into Hank's recorded dream. It takes him a full night to read it through, substituting Hank's dream for his own:
> "The dawn had come when I laid the Manuscript aside. The rain had almost ceased, the world was gray and sad, the exhausted storm was sighing and sobbing itself to rest." He finds Hank ("my stranger") in delirium, adrift in time, and convinced that his starting point, the nineteenth century, was a dream, and that the sixth, where he is "Boss," is the site of "all that could make life worth the living." Nor does Mark Twain give him the lie. Rather, he bends over his stranger and speaks "merely a work, to call attention." The effect is immediate: "His glassy eyes and his ashy face were alight in an instant with pleasure, gratitude, gladness, welcome." We are not told what work it is that Mark Twain whispers. But if it is "Sir Boss," as likely it is, the Twain was confirming not only Hank's belief in the reality of his dream, but his own belief as well—and this in spite of the dark and apocalyptic vision to which his hero had conducted him.

It is possible, and perhaps more interesting, to read aspects of the ending a little differently: As an experiment in literary imagining, Twain and Hank are one. As a psychological exercise, Twain allows Hank the insanity of the dream and retrieves him from the dream when the insanity has let him go. Did he whisper "Sir Boss" into Hank's ear? Like the conversations between Huck and Jim to which we are never privy, this is one of Twain's best jokes: the words that we can never read, the subtext only Twain can know.

In "Unreplying Vacancies: The Disconnected Dialogue of *A Connecticut Yankee in King Arthur's Court*," in *Mark Twain's Ethical Realism: The Aesthetics of Race, Class, and Gender* (1997), Joe Fulton observes that the focus of critical debate centers on the "Battle of the Sand-Belt" and what it may reveal about Twain's stance toward technology. But critics usually ignore the actual end of the novel, "Final P.S. by M.T.," in which Hank, delirious on his deathbed, tries to telephone into the past to speak with the daughter, "Hello-Central," that he left in the sixth century:

> Hello-Central!... She doesn't answer. Asleep, perhaps? Bring her when she wakes, and let me touch her hands, her face, her hair, and tell her good-bye.... Sandy!... Yes, you are there. I lost myself a moment, and I thought you were gone.... Have I been sick long?

The pairing of an inadequate technology and death, Fulton suggests, emphasizes the failure of technology to help us overcome our interpersonal disconnectedness:

> Indeed, the telephone plays a significant role in the novel: Hank's fiancée, Puss Flanagan, had been a "hello-girl," or telephone operator, in Hartford. Hearing Hank's nightmarish attempts to "call" Puss in his sleep, Sandy names their daughter Hello-Central. In a sense, Hank attempts to "call the future" when he finds himself in Camelot, and he goes "calling and harking all up and down the unreplying vacancies of a vanished world" in his dreams. Hank's "disconnected dialogues" strike a new note in Twain's fiction, one that marks the beginning of the more pessimistic Mark Twain of the later years. Unlike *Adventures of Huckleberry Finn*, in which characters willfully "play double" to avoid dialogic interaction, in *Connecticut Yankee*, the switch fails despite Hank Morgan's gradual relaxing of his monologic control.... But Hank, whose voice contains the accents of

both tyranny and democracy, is himself victimized by the
mechanization of language interactions he introduces. In
Connecticut Yankee, Hank designs inventions and technologies
to "connect" people by encouraging dialogue, but he
connects ultimately only with "unreplying vacancies."

Technology and Twain's ambivalence toward it in *Connecticut Yankee* has
attracted much critical attention, but parallels may be drawn between
the "switches" that occur in Camelot and those found in his other
novels:

> These switches address an Arthurian class structure that
> resembles the stratification of Dawson's Landing in
> *Pudd'nhead Wilson*, the various towns of *Adventures of
> Huckleberry Finn*, and, of course, Twain's own childhood
> Hannibal, Missouri, where class lines "were quite clearly
> drawn." In particular, *Connecticut Yankee* recalls *The Prince
> and the Pauper* in its use of English material and in its
> concern for issues of institutionalized class difference. As in
> Twain's other novels, socialization or "training" creates these
> differences and provides the rationale for the switch; the
> switch allows "re-training."
> "Training—training is everything," Hank proclaims....
> Training in Camelot, however, is "petrified training,"
> Hank observes, and more highly institutionalized than any
> example in Twain's other fictional societies. Arthur's
> Camelot, like the Phelps's farm and Dawson's Landing, has
> churches that formalize the stratification of society. But the
> church in *Connecticut Yankee* seems much more sinister and
> all-encompassing....
> ... In *Connecticut Yankee*, laws create a "brickbat culture"
> that limits human freedom.... [T]he church and the
> government join in legally defining the precise stratum of
> society one occupies, establishing an elaborate pecking
> order.... Like the aristocrats of *The Prince and the Pauper* who
> expel the psychosocial other from consciousness by
> considering it "offal," *Connecticut Yankee*'s aristocrats
> consider the lower orders "dirt" and shout "Get you hence!"

when confronted by them. Even the freemen in this brickbat culture are slaves of the law, and Hank observes that one "needs but to hear an aristocrat speak of the classes below him to recognize—and in but indifferently modified measure—the very air and tone of the actual slaveholder." "By sarcasm of law and phrase," Hank observes, "they were freemen."

Despite the fact that Twain was disappointed and disillusioned by the distance between the American ideal and the American real, *Connecticut Yankee* suggests that democracy, though its lessons were soon distorted by Hank, temporarily drunk with technological power, is our best hope against tyranny—and slavery.

Language ultimately reasserts its power and tears from Hank his belief that the "True Word." is his alone. Only he can hear the conversation with his daughter; his marvelous improvements have culminated not in the "Valley of Holiness," but in the "Valley of Hellishness," and Twain's faith in technology to make our lives better has run its course.

After the publication of *Pudd'hnead Wilson*, in which he returned to the broader and more consuming issues of slavery and racism, Twain devoted years to a successful worldwide lecture tour to restore his failed finances. He enjoyed immense popularity and respect, but he would not write another novel.

By the time of his death, Twain had become a singular voice in American literature: "Emerson, Longfellow, Lowell Holmes—I knew them all and all the rest of our sages, poets, seers, critics, humorists;" William Dean Howells recalled in *My Mark Twain* (1910), "[T]hey were like one another and like other literary men; but Clemens was sole, incomparable, the Lincoln of our literature."

WORKS CITED

Cox, James M. *Mark Twain: The Fate of Humor* (Princeton: Princeton UP, 1966).

———. "Remarks on the Sad Initiation of Huckleberry Finn," *Sewanee Review* 62 (July-September 1954) 389–405.

Fisher, Victor. "Huck Finn Reviewed: The Reception of *Huckleberry Finn* in the United States, 1885–97," *American Literary Realism: 1870-1910* 16 (Spring 1983): 1–57.

Florence, Don. "'Gazing Out Over the Ocean of Time': *The Innocents Abroad*," *Persona and Humor in Mark Twain's Early Writings* (Columbia: U Missouri Press, 1995): 62–92.

Fulton, Joe B. *Mark Twain's Ethical Realism: The Aesthetics of Race, Class, and Gender* (Columbia: U Missouri Press, 1997).

Howells, William Dean. *My Mark Twain: Reminiscences and Criticisms* (New York and London, 1910).

Hutchinson, Stuart. "*The Adventures of Tom Sawyer* and *The Adventures of Huckleberry Finn*," *Mark Twain—Humour on the Run* (Atlanta: Editions Rodopi B.V., 1994): 54–63.

Johnson, James L. "A Connecticut Yankee," *Mark Twain and the Limits of Power* (Knoxville: U Tennessee Press, 1982): 120–154.

Morrison, Toni. *Playing in the Dark: Whiteness and the Literary Imagination* (Cambridge, MA, 1992).

Pettit, Arthur G. "Mark Twain and the Negro," *Journal of Negro History* 56 (April 1971): 88–96.

———. "Mark Twain's Attitude Toward the Negro in the West, 1861-67," *The Western Historical Quarterly* 1 (January 1970): 51–62.

Smith, David L. "Huck, Jim, and American Racial Discourse," *Mark Twain Journal* 22 (1984): 4-12.

Turner, Arlin. "Mark Twain and the South: An Affair of Love and Anger," *The Southern Review* 4 (April 1968): 493–519.

Washington, Booker T. "[Tributes to Mark Twain]," *North American Review* 191 (June 1910): 828–30.

Wolff, Cynthia Griffin. "The Adventures of Tom Sawyer: A Nightmare Vision of American Boyhood," *The Massachusetts Review* 21 (Winter 1980): 637–52.

Wonham, Henry B. "Joyous Heresy: Traveling with the Innocent Abroad," *Mark Twain and the Art of the Tall Tale* (NY: Oxford UP, 1993): 70–88.

NEIL SCHMITZ

Mark Twain's Civil War: Humor's Reconstructive Writing

Humor, at its best, forgives and resolves a grievous wrong. It admits it, full measure, receives it, and expresses the immediate experience in humorous language. With verbal dexterity, in some comical voice, it economizes pain's impact. It speaks beautifully in Huck Finn's report of Buck Grangerford's death: "It made me so sick I most fell out of the tree. I ain't agoing to tell all that happened—it would make me sick again if I was to do that. I wished I hadn't ever come ashore that night, to see such things. I ain't ever going to get shut of them—lots of times I dream about them."[1] Humor doesn't deny, or defend; it transacts, it negotiates. Buck is dead, but there's Jim and the blessed raft, safety, survival. The Civil War section of the *Adventures of Huckleberry Finn* ends with Huck's euphoria, the sensation of escape, river and raft sweeping Huck away from the combat zone, ends with Huck's ecstatic rediscovery of Jim, the good food, the great stories. "You feel mighty free and easy and comfortable on a raft" (HF 155). Briefly Huck sails free of the unreconstructed South. Its fight is not his fight. He's not a Grangerford, doesn't see himself in their narrative. His is the new narrative of the new (reconstructed) South, the solution for a still-dumbfounded postbellum Southern writing, very shaky in its postwar fiction, its plots, its speeches.

In 1865 the principal Confederate armies, everywhere either hemmed in by General U. S. Grant or pursued by General W. T.

From *The Cambridge Companion to Mark Twain*, Forrest G. Robinson, ed. (NY: Cambridge University Press, 1995): 74–91. Reprinted by permission of Cambridge University Press.

Sherman, began to suffer major desertion. Manpower shortages were so critical, the Confederate government, in March 1865, too late, began to emancipate slaves for military service. There were casuistical Confederates (Jefferson Davis, Robert E. Lee, Judah Benjamin, Davis's secretary of state) who could parse the irony, but for most Southerners the decision was lunacy, and open admission that the South had lost the argument, lost the right to be at war. Slavery was the "chief stone of the corner," Alexander Stephens, Jefferson Davis's vice-president, had said in 1861. "Be it good or bad, [slavery] has grown up with our society and institutions, and is so interwoven with them, that to destroy it would be to destroy us as a people." This was the hard core of John C. Calhoun's Southern doctrine, the compact center of Southern ideology. "I hold," said Calhoun, "that in the present state of civilization, where two races of different origin, and distinguished by color, and other physical differences, as well as intellectual, are brought together, the relation now existing in the slaveholding states between the two, is, instead of an evil, a good—a positive good."[2] Hard-pressed by Grant and Sherman, unable to see God's favor in the turn of events, the cause seemingly fatally compromised (there was an argument for a selective Confederate emancipation), the Confederate South in 1865 could no longer convincingly assert its nationalist project. What was the expense of life and treasure for? R. M. T. Hunter, Davis's first secretary of state (1861–2), wrote, "I do not see, but I feel, that there is a righteous God in Heaven, who holds our destinies in his hand, and I do not believe He will allow us to be cast down and the wicked to prosper." But He did visibly seem to do so. "What have we done that the Almighty should scourge us with such a war?" General Josiah Gorgas asked in his diary. "Is the cause really hopeless? Is it to be abandoned and lost in this way?"[3] Everywhere there was isolation, stupefaction, silence. "We are shut in here," Mary Chesnut wrote, "turned with our faces to a dead wall. No mails. A letter is sometimes brought by a man on horseback, traveling through the wilderness made by Sherman. All RR's destroyed—bridges gone. We are cut off from the world—to eat out our own hearts."[4]

Substantially revised in the postwar period, 1881–4, but never brought into final book form, Chesnut's Civil War diary, even in its several modern editions, remains a mélange of contradictory thought and feeling. It contains many great lines and passages, but nothing ever adds up, gets larger or deeper, escapes the frame of the daily narrative. It is this massive unfinished text that is the consummate work of revisionary Confederate literature, not the massive finished apologetics of Jefferson Davis's *The Rise and Fall of the Confederate Government* (1881), of Alexander Stephens's *Constitutional View of the Late War Between the States* (1868–70). Chesnut freely expresses what they rigorously exclude in their text-based analyses, the real burden of Confederate nationalism, and does so early on, March 18, 1861.

> I wonder if it be a sin to think slavery a curse to any land. Sumner said not one word of this hated institution which is not true. Men and women are punished when their masters and mistresses are brutes and not when they do wrong and then we live surrounded by prostitutes. An abandoned woman is sent out of any decent house elsewhere. Who thinks any worse of a negro or mulatto woman for being a thing we can't name? God forgive us, but ours is a monstrous system and wrong and iniquity.

Unlike Harriet Beecher Stowe, whom she read with hateful admiration, Chesnut couldn't locate a motive, moral, or plot for this antislavery position in her daily narrative. It was, after all, the damage slavery did to the marriages of respectable Southern white women that principally appalled her. "Thank God for my countrywomen," she writes in this same entry, "—alas for the men! No worse than men everywhere, but the lower their mistresses, the more degraded they must be." She didn't see the self-centeredness of her antislavery position in the sixties, and didn't see it in the eighties. "My Molly," her personal slave, exits the diary in June 1865, saying, "Never lef' Missis for no husband an' children in this world."[5] "My Molly" says it all. This Confederate trope, Confederate Southern writing won't surrender.

What was her politics? What is the vision that informs her daily narrative? Chesnut scrupulously reported her reading: *Uncle Tom's Cabin*, Emerson, European histories, English and French literature. Whatever slavery was, monstrous or beautiful, the early narrative of Confederate nationalism brought to mind great histories, epic deeds. "While I was cudgeling my brain to say what kind of men we ought to choose," she writes in 1861, "I fell on Clarendon, and it was easy to construct my man out of this material." Many Confederates in 1861–2

looked into the *History of the Rebellion and the Civil Wars in England*
(1702–4), pondered the mix of identifications: Cavalier/Puritan,
tyranny/rebellion, Charles I/Cromwell. What story—English, biblical,
classical—explained Southern defeat in 1865? At the end Chesnut was
reading Byron's *Childe Harold's Pilgrimage*; Carlyle's *The French
Revolution*, especially chapter 4, "The Loser Pays"; Sylvio Pellico's *Le
Mie Prigioni* (1832), a political prisoner account; and Thomas Hood's
"The Bridge of Sighs" (1844). In the C. Vann Woodward 1981 edition
of Chesnut's diary, Mary Chesnut says finally, "Forgiveness is
indifference. Forgiveness is impossible while *love lasts*." She quotes
Hood: "Make no deep scrutiny / Into our mutiny—."[6]

As Chesnut toiled over her diaries in the early 1880s, wanting
dramatic coherence and intensity, wanting, but failing, to find a witty,
far-seeing Cassandra in her text, the figure of conceptual order, a supple
reconstructed Southern humorous writing came suddenly into the field
and produced the first significant Southern reading of the Civil War.
George Washington Cable's *The Grandissimes* (1880), Joel Chandler
Harris's *Uncle Remus: His Songs and His Sayings* (1881), Mark Twain's
Adventures of Huckleberry Finn (1884), Thomas Nelson Page's *In Ole
Virginia* (1887) are interested in forgiveness, accept the humiliation and
subjection of the Confederate South, undertake a therapy of disclosure,
offer effective strategies of displacement and insulation, do the work of
humor. Confederate generals surrendered to Grant and Sherman. These
Southern writers surrendered to Harriet Beecher Stowe. Uncle Tom was
the opportune figure, his text, his speech, the place where the
unspeakable (trust) could be entertained, the impossible (love) regarded.
"My Molly" is fairly silent in Confederate writing, restricted in her
speech. Uncle Tom speaks volumes, is the fount of story. He was the site
of knowledge, where the deepest South revealed itself. Harris had put it
together beautifully, the mis-en-scène, the words:

> One night, while the little boy was watching Uncle Remus
> twisting and waxing some shoe-thread, he made what
> appeared to him to be a very curious discovery. He
> discovered that the palms of the old man's hands were as
> white as his own, and the fact was such a source of wonder
> that he at last made it the subject of a remark. The response
> of Uncle Remus led to the earnest recital of a piece of

unwritten history that must prove interesting to ethnologists.

"Tooby sho de pa'm er my han's w'ite, honey," he quietly remarked, "en, w'en it comes ter dat, dey wuz a time w'en all de w'ite folks 'uz black—blacker dan me, kaze I done bin yer so long dat I bin sorter bleach out."[7]

All the principal Southern humorists (ethnologists of color and color differences) knew how brilliant this was, this kind of writing with its tender exchanges, how appropriate the form and language. Here was a resource, fresh, interesting, extensive, a history not yet written, the turn Chesnut could not make, to My Molly, her subjectivity, her history.

In the 1880s, Mark Twain and Cable toured together, giving readings and lectures. Harris would have toured with them, but he had a fear of public speaking. When Page toured, he, too, wanted Uncle Remus in the act, and couldn't get him. All were variously published in the same powerful Northern journals and magazines, often in the same issue. Harris and Page remained within the conceit of the sentimental, were formally and tonally reassuring whatever the grief their fiction bore. Page was the most sedative of the humorists. "Dem wuz good ole times, marster—de bes' Sam ever see! Dey wuz, in fac'! Niggers didn' hed nothin' 't all to do—jes' hed to 'ten' to de feedin' an' cleanin' de hosses an' doin' what de marster tell 'em to do; an' when dey wuz sick, dey had things sont 'em out de house, an' de same doctor come to see 'em what 'ten to de white folks when dey wuz po'ly."[8] The stories his black storytellers typically tell are about their beloved masters and mistresses, "Marse Chan" and "Meh Lady: A Story of the War" in *Ole Virginia*. In Harris's text, the fable's frame, Uncle Remus's tender care of Miss Sally's seven-year-old boy, held the turbulent feelings set forth in the stories. "Food-sharing, sex-sharing—the Remus stories read like a catalogue of Southern racial taboos, all standing on their heads," Bernard Wolfe tells us in his superb 1949 essay on Harris. "It was the would-be novelist in him who created Remus, the 'giver' of interracial caresses, but the trained journalist in him, having too good an eye and ear, reported the energetic folk blow in the caress."[9] Mark Twain and Cable set Stowe's figure and conceit at risk in different ways, confronted larger issues in their fiction. In *The Grandissimes*, where it is 1803–4, the lynching of a black woman, Clemence, is briefly described in cold documentary prose.

Of these writers, Mark Twain is the most problematic, the most distanced from the New South championed in Henry Woodfin Grady's *Atlanta Constitution*, a New South that still venerated its Confederate fathers, still insisted: "The South has nothing for which to apologize." Grady's famous 1886 speech, "The New South," given at a banquet in New York, spelled out the New South's perfect understanding of the prime dictate of Unionist discourse. It listened, this triumphant Unionist discourse, to Southern protestation, and then it asked: "But what of the negro?" The New South, Grady assured his public, understood what was to be done. "Our future, our very existence depends upon our working out this problem in full and equal justice." It affirmed the Unionist discourse of Lincoln and Sherman, their definitive versions. "We understand that when Lincoln signed the emancipation proclamation, your victory was assured, for he then committed you to the cause of human liberty, against which the arms of man cannot prevail—(while those of our statesmen who trusted to make slavery the corner-stone of the Confederacy doomed us to defeat as far as they could, committing us to a cause that reason could not defend or the sword maintain in the sight of advancing civilization)." The New South went this far into Unionist discourse, but had its reservations, its obstinacies. At certain critical instances, the Confederate and Unionist narratives were still in conflict. The "late struggle between the States was war and not rebellion, revolution and not conspiracy." As Grady had it, the "new South presents a perfect democracy, the oligarchs leading in the popular movement." There were problems and paradoxes everywhere in Grady's speech, as there were in the New South itself. How does oligarchical democracy so perfectly work? What now was the status of black people in the New South? Of Harris's Uncle Remus and Page's Sam, the black men the New South chose to recognize and celebrate, it said: "To liberty and enfranchisement is as far as the law can carry the negro. The rest must be left to conscience and common sense." Harris wrote for the *Atlanta Constitution*, was its principal editorial writer. Why couldn't Harris do public readings of his Uncle Remus stories? In *Life on the Mississippi* (1883), Mark Twain saw through Harris's shyness, saw the whole rich irony of the New South's situation in Unionist discourse, of its humorous transactions in dialect poetry.

> [Harris] deeply disappointed a number of children who
> flocked eagerly to Mr. Cable's house to get a glimpse of the

illustrious sage and oracle of the nation's nurseries. They said:

"Why, he's white!"

They were grieved about it. So, to console them, the book was brought, that they might hear Uncle Remus's Tar-baby story from the lips of Uncle Remus himself—or what, in their outraged eyes, was left of him. But it turned out that he had never read aloud to people, and was too shy to venture the attempt now.[10]

Mark Twain, it might be said, was the Southern humorist gone over, not just a deserter, a dissenter, but a literary scalawag, a Southern writer in Unionist discourse and narrative. Chapter 6 in Louis Budd's *Mark Twain: Social Philosopher* (1962) is entitled "The Scalawag." As Budd has it, this heavy term (its modern cognates are "quisling," "collaborator") aptly characterizes Mark Twain's political practice in the postwar period. There he was, at all those postwar Grand Army of the Republic banquets, happily toasting Union generals. The *Notice* posted at the head of *Huckleberry Finn* evokes Civil War/Reconstruction orders, the bills put up in the courthouse squares of occupied Southern cities and towns. "Persons attempting to find a moral in it will be banished; persons attempting to find a plot in it will be shot." For all its Southern speech, this text is in Unionist discourse. It abjures Sir Walter Scott, professes Uncle Tom.

How did Mark Twain get here, and how secure, how satisfying, is Huck's position? As late as 1954, the New South was still warily regarding Mark Twain. In his compendious *The South in American Literature, 1607–1900* (1954), Jay B. Hubbell, deriding Mark Twain's Scott thesis, argued that "Mark Twain had been out of touch with Southern life so long that, like many Northern travelers and historians, he had come to look for some simple formula which would explain the many differences between the two sections." As for Mark Twain's Jim: "There is in his picture of slavery a little too much of the old abolitionist legend of the Deep South."[11] I count as the classic texts in Mark Twain's Civil War writing "A True Story" (1874), *Life on the Mississippi* (1883), *Huckleberry Finn* (1885), and "The Private History of a Campaign That Failed" (1885). Mark Twain's reconstructive humorous reading of the Civil War gets essentially done in these texts, which were published in important national magazines—the *Atlantic Monthly*, the *Century Illustrated Monthly Magazine*—and immediately entered the major discursive networks in American literature. "An Adventure of Huckleberry Finn: With an Account of the Famous Grangerford-Shepherdson Feud" appeared in the November 1884 issue of the *Century*, which had just begun its monumental series, *Battles and Leaders of the Civil War*. Readers turned past Huck's account of Buck Grangerford's death, past E. W. Kemble's illustration, "Behind the Woodpile" (Grangerford farm boys shooting at Shepherdson farm boys), to find Warren Lee Goss's mud gritty "Recollections of a Private" and its illustration, a mounted federal cavalryman. It put Mark Twain figuratively right in the thick of things, though up a tree, onlooking, *hors de combat*.

To enter the cultural debate over the remembrance and meaning of the Civil War, to ponder the responsibility of the South for the Civil War, Mark Twain had bravely to come forward and admit he had no right to speak about such matters. He had spent the Civil War in Nevada, a sometime employee of the federal government, most of the time advancing his career as a comic journalist. What was he doing at all these military banquets, loving the toasts, the banter, the badinage, the blue coats and brass buttons? Mark Twain's love for the company of old soldiers betrayed him. His voice in this assembly of speakers, he realized, was "a sort of voice,—not a loud one, but a modest one; not a boastful one, but an apologetic one."[12] As early as 1877, in the Putnam Phalanx Dinner Speech, delivered in Hartford, Mark Twain had begun to address, humorously, at once the painful issue of his desertion and the present problem of his right to speak about the Civil War. "I did not assemble at the hotel parlors today to be received by a committee as a mere civilian guest; no, I assembled at the headquarters of the Putnam Phalanx, and insisted upon my right to be escorted to this place as one of the military guests. For I, too, am a soldier! I am inured to war. I have a military history."[13] This, too, was a sort of voice, facetious, protected.

"Putnam Phalanx" is the first draft of "The Private History of a Campaign That Failed," a suspiciously breezy first draft oozing anxiety. There is no traumatic shooting in this first piece. It is Ben Tupper, not young Samuel Clemens, who boyishly rationalizes his desertion: "Gentlemen, you can do as you choose; as for me, I've got enough of this sashaying around so's 't you can't get a chance to pray, because the time's all required for cussing" (MTS 108). And there was, too, as Justin Kaplan taught us in *Mr. Clemens and Mark Twain* (1966), the complex issue of Mark Twain's relation to U. S. Grant, the question "why a former Confederate irregular should be publishing, and ostensibly making a good deal of money doing so, the *Personal Memoirs* of the commander of all the Union armies."[14] In 1887, two years after the publication of the "Private History," addressing the Union Veterans Association of Maryland, Mark Twain was at his boldest: "You Union veterans of Maryland have prepared your feast and offered to me, a rebel veteran of Missouri, the wound-healing bread and salt of a gracious hospitality" (MTS 219). Tom Quirk and Richard E. Peck have written excellent essays on the relation of *Huckleberry Finn* to the "Private History." "This moving tale of Clemens shooting a stranger," Peck writes, "is, if you like, a lie, a most useful lie because it pulls into focus all the fragments comprising 'The History' in a dramatic conclusion that accounts for (and 'justifies'?) Clemens' desertion on grounds that it represented a moral act."[15] Yet there is a difference between young Samuel Clemens's retreat from his wartime duty in the Marion Rangers, his desertion of the cause of Confederate nationalism, and Huck's flight. *Huckleberry Finn* is not only about running away, it is also about the fright and guilt of changing sides.

In these Civil War texts, "A True Story," *Life on the Mississippi*, *Huckleberry Finn*, and "Private History," Mark Twain looks for ways to break out of the Southern imaginary (William Gilmore Simms, Sidney Lanier) into a Northern real (William Dean Howells, U. S. Grant), to break its narcissistic Sir Walter Scott trance, to open his text to the real, to difference, to the most radical of alterities. "Sir Walter," Mark Twain wrote in *Life on the Mississippi*, "had so large a hand in making Southern character, as it existed before the war, that he is in great measure responsible for the war. It seems a little harsh toward a dead man to say that we never should have had any war but for Sir Walter; and yet something of a plausible argument might, perhaps, be made in support of that wild proposition."[16] The Scott chapter is entitled "Enchantments and Enchanters." As Mark Twain saw it, there was no longer a usable Southern patriarchal literary tradition, a Confederate narrative. There was just the biracial Southern narrative Harriet Beecher Stowe had mothered in American literature, its complexities, its dreads, its horrors. Huck is in Unionist discourse, but only because where Jim is going, what Jim wants, is the Ohio, not the Mississippi. Such is the breakthrough of *Huckleberry Finn*, its stroke of genius. With Huck, Mark Twain sort of deserts Tom Sawyer, sort of chooses Jim. Mark Twain is a Southern writer in Unionist discourse, happily at work within its tenets, but always revising its terms, exploring its tolerances, its shortcomings, its practical meaning. Huck's speech is equivocal. His narrative isn't yet committed to a direction, isn't totally invested in a denouement. Hence we see in Mark Twain's Civil War writing this ongoing literary phenomenon, narratives interrupted, invaded, silenced. Huck is always on the move, now in Tom's story, then in Jim's, just as Tom and Jim come upon Huck's story and try to determine it. Huck's narrative is afloat, in passive suspense. Whose story is told here? Huck's? Tom's? Jim's? Humor reaches here its purest liquidity, its supplest resilience. What does Huck's speech do? It registers, it goes on.

All this discourse shifting and story breaching in *Huckleberry Finn* is remarkably foretold in "A True Story," which warns us about reading Jim as Uncle Remus, seeing in him what Misto C sees in Aunt Rachel: "She was a cheerful, hearty soul, and it was no more trouble for her to laugh than it is for a bird to sing."[17] The interlocutor is a Northern liberal gentleman who didn't request the story he receives, doesn't even want to hear it. "Why, I thought—that is, I meant—why, you *can't* have had any trouble. I've never heard you sigh, and never seen your eye when there wasn't a laugh in it" (TS 60). The title, "A True Story, Repeated Word for Word as I Heard It," still marks his incredulity and denial, as a Northerner, of any involvement or responsibility for Aunt Rachel's "trouble." He is here only as a scene setter, as asking the provocative question, as putting into play the decisive term, "trouble." It is in fact the outrageous ignorance/innocence of the interlocutor's casual remark that abruptly cuts Aunt Rachel's uproarious laughter off. "Aunt Rachel, how is it that you've lived sixty years and never had any trouble?" It is the lie of the euphemism that gives Aunt Rachel her sudden stab of pain, that snaps into sharp focus her relation to Misto C and his family, her alienated difference. "Trouble" is Misto C's cloaking term for slavery, his denial of its experience and its consequences. *How is it you're so merry— you who were once a slave? Slavery could not have been that bad since it has left you the joyous creature you are.* As the sketch begins, Aunt Rachel is "sitting respectfully below our level, on the steps,—for she was our servant, and colored." Into the narration of her story, word for word as he heard it, the interlocutor intrudes only once more, to reset the scene of narration. "Aunt Rachel had gradually risen, while she warmed to her subject, and now she towered above us, black against the stars" (TS 60). It has been an after-dinner sit on the porch, summertime, twilight, the company has been teasing Aunt Rachel, entertained by the rich exuberance of her Negro mirth, and then that explosively wrong phrase is uttered, "and never had any trouble." "Has I had any trouble? Misto C—, I's gwine to tell you, den I leave it to you" (TS 59–60). After Aunt Rachel towers, black against the stars, the interlocutor disappears. Aunt Rachel has the closing, the conversion of Misto C's term. "Oh, no, Misto C—, I hain't had no trouble. An' no *joy!*" (TS 63). This sentence is like a freeze-frame, Misto C's term in a wreckage of negatives.

To this extent, "A True Story" prefigures certain transactions in *Huckleberry Finn*, especially those in the pre-Cairo chapters. Jim will also speak up here, emerge in his threatening difference and counter Huck vigorously. "Doan talk to me 'bout Sollermun, Huck, I knows him by de back" (HF 95). "A True Story" thus redirects Southern writing, turns comic dialect sketch into serious testimony, a survivor's tale told in "'arnest," and does so with artful tact, inscribing the narrator's flawed appropriation, even though Aunt Rachel gives her story to him, leaves it with him. In that framework, Mark Twain's "A True Story" testifies to the literary value of Aunt Rachel's testimony. It realizes, as it were, that all the emergent complexities of African-American experience, the riches of its oral tradition, *His Songs and His Sayings* (Harris's subtitle), are properly the resources of Southern literature, as long as the Anglo-American writer inscribes Misto C. Liberated, enabled, this Southern writing already occupies in 1874 the fictive space Toni Morrison has come to define in *Song of Solomon* (1977) and *Beloved* (1987), African-American family history at the critical juncture of emancipation.

What are the familial traces? What are the documentary texts? In "A True Story," there is just a saying. A grandmother born in Maryland, a proud woman, would say: "I wa'nt bawn in de mash to be fool'd by trash. I's one o' de old Blue Hen's Chickens." And a scar, to recognize. Aunt Rachel's son, "my little Henry tore his wris' awful, and most busted his head, right up at de top of his forehead, an' de niggers didn't fly aroun' fas' enough to 'tend him" (TS 60). The grandmother angrily declares her saying, clears the kitchen, bandages the child's wounds. The family is sold at auction, broken up. Aunt Rachel loses her husband and her seven children. "—an' six of 'em I hain't set eyes on ag'in to dis day, an' dat's twenty-two years ago las' Easter" (TS 61). When the Civil War comes, African-Americans begin searching for each other, children for parents, parents for children. Henry, who had run North and prospered, "sole out an' went to whar dey was recruitin,' an' hired hisse'f out to de colonel for his servant; an' den he went all froo de battles everywhah, huntin' for his ole mammy" (TS 62). Saying and scar are finally matched, mother and son, a family line established, but there are ominous complications. A "*nigger* ridgment" on guard at the mansion where Aunt Rachel manages the kitchen holds a dance in that kitchen. Henry doesn't recognize his mother, treats her insolently, "smilin' at my big red turban, and makin' fun," has an attitude not unlike Misto C's, whereupon Aunt Rachel indignantly uses the grandmother's saying. In the rapture of the reunion, Aunt Rachel briefly exults: "Lord God ob heaven be praise,' I got my own ag'in!" But what then? Where is she now? Where is Henry? "A True Story," as we've seen, abruptly closes.

"A True Story" gives us summarily an African-American account of the American midcentury, the 1850s, the Civil War, the Reconstruction. The three actions in *Huckleberry Finn* refer to these periods in Southern history. In the first section, chapters 1–16, written largely in 1876, runaway Huck suddenly finds himself in a slave narrative, a secondary character, reluctantly, anxiously, aiding and abetting Jim's flight to freedom in Illinois. We are here in actual time, in the 1850s. The middle section, chapters 16–22, written in 1879–80, begins with the Grangerford–Shepherdson feud, the chapter Mark Twain purposefully dealt into the series, *Battles and Leaders of the Civil War*, and ends with the humiliating overthrow of the king and the duke. The final section, chapters 31-43, written in 1883, concerns setting free an already freed Jim, symbolically enacts the Reconstruction as a nightmarish agony. For us the problem is the middle section, its gunfire, its bands and mobs of men. In this section we come upon the South as a place, a people, a nationality. Of the sections, it is the riskiest. It exposes Huck up his tree, keeps him in constant jeopardy, puts him in that hard place where he must finally choose sides. At these points, *Huckleberry Finn* intersects with *Life on the Mississippi*, with Mark Twain's reminiscences of his Civil War experience: "Putnam Phalanx," "Private History," "An Author's Soldiering." Complexes of pacifist/bellicose feeling swirl through the middle section of *Huckleberry Finn*. What is courage? The Grangerford episode seems to say one thing, the Bricksville episode another, the Wilks episode still another.

"The new South is simply the old South under new conditions."[18] In its ideological negotiation with the North, Grady's New South insisted that it be allowed to sanctify the memory of the old regime. "The sign of nobility in her families for generations to come will be the gray cap or the stained coat, on which, in the ebb of losing battle, God laid the sword of his imperishable knighthood." The New South would be progressive, would be in Unionist discourse, but it wouldn't recant, wouldn't criticize the fathers. "Slavery as an institution cannot be defended—but its administration was so nearly perfect among our forefathers as to challenge and hold our loving respect."[19] There is a lot of bad faith oozing in Grady's formulations; "its administration" simply lies on the page, blatant, palpable. The Confederate fathers "administered" slavery, and did the work of it so well as to "hold our loving respect." Could one retain Confederate articles, Confederate tropes, in Unionist discourse, perhaps even revise Unionist discourse, end the insistence of its punishing question: "But what of the negro?" In its early going, Grady's New South, Harris its principal writer, struggled with this question, worked in a humorous mode to resolve it. The human slaves and masters in Page's *Old Virginia* are the very Brers in Harris's *Uncle Remus*. Slavery is foregrounded, sentimentalized. The newspaper that brings the tragic news of Lincoln's assassination to old Colonel Cameron in D. W. Griffith's *Birth of a Nation* (1915) is the *New South*, the name boldly printed. Griffith's film epic, which beautifully illustrates the jam and the jar of the two narratives, Confederate and Unionist, is at its most gloriously appropriative creating a Confederate Lincoln, a Lincoln sort of compelled to sign the Emancipation Proclamation.

Bad faith in *Huckleberry Finn* is rankest in the middle section. In the Old South you can't live without it, Huck discovers, offering that knowledge to us as a truism. "If they wanted us to call them kings and dukes, I hadn't no objections, 'long as it would keep peace in the family; and it warn't no use to tell Jim, so I didn't tell him. If I never learnt nothing else out of pap, I learnt that the best way to get along with his kind of people is to let them have their own way" (HF 165). Forrest G. Robinson writes, in *In Bad Faith: The Dynamics of Deception in Mark Twain's America* (1986), a dark Melvillean reading of *Huckleberry Finn*,

"Bad Faith rules, by necessity, in all human affairs." Huck's phrase, "no use," is particularly telling. "Perhaps Huck's decision not to tell is the reflex of his fear that Jim will react to the truth by running away; perhaps, too, it expresses a fatalistic surrender to the inevitable failure of the quest. Whatever the case, the 'no use' that Huck appeals to cannot possibly speak for Jim, even though in declining to share what he knows Huck does just that."[20] No use, *now*. We are in and out of faiths, and narratives, in *Huckleberry Finn*. Jim, too, is withholding information. He has not told Huck that the reason for his flight no longer exists, that the cruel, murderous Pap Finn who is after Huck is dead. In the Old South of *Huckleberry Finn*, in the New South of *Life on the Mississippi*, everywhere, even among the best of friends, there is, at times, serious bad faith, significant withholding.

In what ways does the middle of *Huckleberry Finn*, so heavily freighted with Civil War experience, the bad feeling of that bad faith, humorously resolve its subject? Bad acting, always before us, is a major trope. The circus gives us good acting, we briefly see it, the fake drunk is a real acrobat, Huck is amazed, and then it is gone. The king and the duke, fabulators, mythologists, confidence men, bad actors, are in specific relation to those other two bad actors, Colonel Grangerford and Colonel Sherburn. These rule Huck's world, shore and river, in the middle section. Colonel Grangerford commands foolhardy courage, life-wasting bravery. Colonel Sherburn confronts riotous bravado, personal cowardice. They wear the planter's white suit, the white suit that would in time become Mark Twain's signature suit. When Colonel Sherburn speaks, Mark Twain forces his way into Huck's text. It is the worst moment in *Huckleberry Finn*. Suddenly there is ugly writing, conflicted feeling, unresolved thinking, a spew of angry statements. It is as if Colonel Sherburn were addressing the Marion Rangers of "Private History." "But a mob without any *man* at the head of it, is *beneath* pitifulness. Now the thing for you to do, is to droop your tails and go home and crawl in a hole" (HF 191). Buck Grangerford, on the other hand, is ready to die, and his father is too. "I don't like that shooting from behind a bush," Colonel Grangerford tells thirteen-year-old Buck. "Why didn't you step into the road, my boy?" (HF 145). This is bad acting, as is the shooting of Buck floundering in the river, unable to defend himself, unarmed, in the open. But it is the king and the duke, the doctors of divinity and literature, who are always before us in the middle section, who deliver, at once lunatic and fraudulent, the ongoing dominant discourse.

In *Life on the Mississippi* Sir Walter Scott is the name of that discourse, of its romantic *a priori*, its faux medievalism. Scott enchains Southern thinking, Southern imagining, "with decayed and swinish forms of religion; with decayed and degraded systems of government; with the sillinesses and emptinesses, sham grandeurs, sham gauds, and sham chivalries of a brainless and worthless long-vanished society" (LM 241). He "made every gentleman in the South a major or a colonel, or a general or a judge, before the war," created "rank and caste down there, and also reverence for rank and caste, and pride and pleasure in them" (LM 242). He is the progenitor, the forefather, his faux medievalism the enabling mythos, its theology, its poetry. He is the killer of Southern writing. There is strenuous pursuit of Sir Walter Scott in *Life on the Mississippi*. Mark Twain stresses his radical disaffiliation. Chapter 46, "Enchantments and Enchanters," is the hottest chapter in the book, and still seething. Here, too, Mark Twain curiously inscribes the feminine, puts a mark on the manliness of Southern chivalry. "Take away the romantic mysteries, the kings and knights and big-sounding titles, and Mardi Gras would die, down there in the South. The very feature that keeps it alive—girly-girly romance—would kill it in the North or in London" (LM 241–2). In *Huckleberry Finn* the Duke of Bridgewater has about him a certain effeminacy, a certain intonation. Rehearsing the king as Juliet, the duke says: "You mustn't bellow out *Romeo!* that way, like a bull—you must say it soft, and sick, and languishy, so—R-o-o-meo! that is the idea; for Juliet's a dear sweet mere child of a girl, you know, and she don't bray like a jackass" (HF 177). It is there in the way the duke calls Looy the Seventeen by his familiar name, Capet, a misnomer, of course. The duke's carpetbag is much more interesting than the king's, which yields, besides clothes, only a "ratty deck of cards." The duke's bag is packed with convenient wonders, posters, costumes, wigs, theatrical face paint. The interesting question of how this squirmy bad acting relates to the straight bad acting of the Grangerfords and Sherburns Mark Twain merely exposes.

On board the raft, the king and the duke immediately establish rank and caste, place and position. Like Sir Walter Scott, they are blissfully blind to the plights of Huck and Jim. The king's first move as the executor of the Wilks estate is to sell the slaves, "two sons up the river to Memphis, and their mother down the river to Orleans" (HF 234). The duke's line: "jour printer, by trade; do a little in patent medicines; theatre-actor—tragedy, you know; take a turn at mesmerism and phrenology when there's a chance; teach singing-geography school for a change; sting a lecture, sometimes." The king's line: "I've done considerable in the doctoring way in my time. Layin' on o' hands is my best holt—for cancer and paralysis, and sich things; and I k'n tell a fortune pretty good, when I've got somebody along to find out the facts for me. Preachin's my line, too; and workin' camp-meetin's; and missionaryin' around" (HF 160–1). Mark Twain's critique of the patriarchal orders in Southern society is encompassing, though differently established. Huck merely registers the moral idiocy of the honor-bound colonels, the casualties of their disastrous leadership, then turns from them, to Jim and the raft, to a circus. He promptly sees through the king and the duke, discounts their fictions, despises their bad acting. Sir Walter Scott is a sunk concern in *Huckleberry Finn*.

In the Wilks episode, the sides are perfectly clear. Huck and Jim have come together on the issue of the king and the duke, shared their detestation of the "rapscallions." Yet Colonel Sherburn is still at large in the text, fearless, contemptuous, a figure not wholly in the brackets of censure, his speech not completely in Sir Walter Scott. He has killed a man with cool dispatch. He stares down Buck Harkness in the crowd, chooses Buck to confront individually. His challenge is—personal cowardice. He cocks his gun. Here's another Buck to be shot. "The crowd washed back sudden, and then broke apart and went tearing off every which way, and Buck Harkness he heeled it after them, looking tolerable cheap" (HF 191). Huck witnesses, makes the barest commentary: "I could a staid, if I'd a wanted to, but I didn't want to" (HF 191). Sherburn is not mentioned again in the narrative. The Colonel, so to speak, goes unanswered—until, that is, Mark Twain's ingeniously worked-out formal response in the "Private History" appears in the *Century*, speaks modestly, humorously, among the war papers in its ongoing Civil War series.

Humor works very hard in this reminiscence. The text argues that it is autobiographical, to be held to the rules of evidence, but does so teasingly, is facetious from the start. There is still something smarmy about the "Private History," something totally unconvincing. It wants to make a pacifist argument (Huck's), wants to represent all the deserters, the Bull Run runners, the rabbits, the Buck Harknesses, the Hucks. It wants to show that Mark Twain left the war because, like Huck, he was horrified by killing, hated killing, but it can't finally face down its Colonel Sherburn, the grimly fearless, coolly self-controlled U. S. Grant. It turns abruptly from the pacifist pieties given over the corpse of the slain stranger to glorify Grant and the killing power of well-trained modern troops. The narrator exits with a nonsequitur, humorously put, cowardly speech par excellence, spoken from the safety of the subjunctive: "I could have become a soldier myself, if I had waited. I had got part of it learned; I knew more about retreating than the man that invented retreating" (PH 123). It echoes Huck's "I could a staid, if I'd a wanted to, but I didn't want to," but differently, is apologizing where Huck is not, is obsequious where Huck is simply decisive. In the text generally, extenuators and specifiers are not always immediately detectable. Here Mark Twain explains his family's relation to slavery: "I said, in palliation of this dark fact, that I had heard my father say, some years before he died, that slavery was a great wrong, and that he would free the solitary negro he then owned if he could think it right to give away the property of the family when he was so straitened in means" (PH 207). "Then" is the fixer in that sentence. The father in fact once dealt in slaves. As for the lugubrious death scene, Mark Twain scholarship has yet to corroborate its actual happening.

"In confronting that past in which the nation had reached its limits and been rent asunder, Mark Twain reached the limits of his humor, which is to say he reached the threshold of his disillusion." James M. Cox's reading of the situation in *Mark Twain: The Fate of Humor* (1966) still stands. "In *Huckleberry Finn* [Mark Twain] had come as near—and as far—as he was ever to do in reconstructing the Civil War past. The 'Private History' marked a second effort to encounter that past, but it was a smaller, safer effort."[21] Humor doesn't pull it off in the "Private History," is uncertain in its focus, doesn't admit the pain, evades it, puts into play the defense of the dead stranger, prevaricates, is contradictory. In *Huckleberry Finn*, Mark Twain's humor works purposefully. Huck says: "I reckon a body that ups and tells the truth when he is in a tight place, is taking considerable many resks; though I ain't had no experience, and can't say for certain; but it looks so to me, anyway; and yet here's a case where I'm blest if it don't look like the truth is better, and actuly *safer*, than a lie" (HF 139). Such is the difference between Huck Finn and

Mark Twain. Huck never signed up, never pledged allegiance to Confederate nationalism. He is its witness, the doings of Sir Walter Scott, of the king and the duke. In the middle section, Huck has already, to some extent, gone over into Jim's narrative. Jim tells him the pitiful story of his deaf child, 'Lizabeth. He has a son, we learn, Johnny. This brief story from Jim's family history is beautifully arresting, and not at all self-serving. Huck will side, too, with Mary Jane Wilks and work to restore the African-American family the king has so callously broken up. This is where he comes into Unionist discourse, specifically into the allegiances of the Stowe variant. Huck signs up for women and blacks. Confiding in Mary Jane, spelling out a very complicated anti-king and duke strategy, Huck manfully swears his oath: "I don't want nothing more out of you than just your word—I'd druther have it than another man's kiss-the-Bible" (HF 239).

Apart from the problematic "Private History," Mark Twain's only other Civil War narrative is in *Life on the Mississippi*, "Vicksburg during the Trouble." Distinctly anti-Confederate, the chapter begins citing the euphemistic term "Trouble," uses the form of the dialect sketch again to do something like a documentary interview. There is no glorification of Confederate heroism here. Under bombardment, frantic women and children scurry for the cave shelters, "encouraged by the humorous grim soldiery, who shout 'Rats, to your holes!' and laugh" (LM 195). A civilian survivor of the siege, a married man, the father of children, remembers, in a flat prosaic voice, the awful tedium, and terror, of bomb-shelter life. He speaks, like Huck, in the language of reportage, seeing it all as it is, marking the absurdities. His wife, Maria, is caught outside as a bombardment begins. "When she was running for the holes, one morning, through a shell shower, a big shell burst near her and covered her all over with dirt, and a piece of iron carried away her game-bag of false hair from the back of her head. Well, she stopped to get that game-bag before she shoved along again!" (LM 196). Humor works very hard here, telling these funny truths. Another time a shell burst interrupts the narrator's inviting a friend to share a drink of rare whisky in his shelter. "A chunk of it cut the man's arm off, and left it dangling in my hand. And do you know the thing that is going to stick longest in my memory, and outlast everything else, little and big, I reckon, is the mean thought I had then? It was, 'the whisky is *saved!*'" (LM 197). In "Vicksburg during the Trouble," humor is almost exhausted, almost becomes the steeled irony of Stephen Crane and Ernest Hemingway, yet not quite, because it is the victim, the survivor who speaks, not the interlocutory observer. "We always had eight; eight belonged there. Hunger and misery and sickness and fright and sorrow, and I don't know what all, got so loaded into them that none of them were ever rightly their old selves after the siege. They all died but three of us within a couple of years" (LM 196).

Mark Twain admires the National Cemetery outside Vicksburg, a "Mount Auburn" cemetery, modern, its grounds "tastefully laid out in broad terraces, with winding roads and paths; and there is a profuse adornment in the way of semitropical shrubs and flowers; and in one part is a piece of native wild-wood, left just as it grew, and, therefore, perfect in its charm" (LM 198). He particularly admires the touch of that remnant piece of wild-wood, "left just as it grew." There is no question here of Mark Twain's chosen side, his respect for the reach and power of the national government, its situation of this National Cemetery, its management of it. "The government's work is always conspicuous for excellence, solidity, thoroughness, neatness. The government does its work well in the first place, and then takes care of it" (LM 198). Unionist discourse empowers him, braces its monuments with metal, lets him interview outside the National Cemetery, an "aged colored man," another survivor of the siege. He

> showed us, with pride, an unexploded bombshell which had lain in his yard since the day it fell during the siege.
>
> "I was a-stannin' heah, an' de dog was a-stannin' heah; de dog he went for de shell, gwine to pick a fuss wid it; but I didn't; I says, 'Jes' make youseff at home heah; lay still whah you is, or bust up de place, jes' as you's a mind to, but *I's* got business out in de woods, *I* has!" (LM 198)

Unionist discourse was multifarious, supple, differently interested, competent in diverse speech. When "a Southerner of genius writes modern English," Mark Twain insisted, "his book goes upon crutches no longer, but upon wings; and they carry it swiftly all about America and England, and through the great English reprint publishing-houses of Germany—as witness the experience of Mr. Cable and 'Uncle Remus,' two of the very few Southern authors who do not write in the Southern style" (LM 243).

Life on the Mississippi is a charter for a new postwar Southern writing, *Huckleberry Finn* its first local masterpiece. Such writing abjures Sir Walter Scott, professes Huck and Jim. But what happens to Harris, to Cable? Only Page, the most apologetic, the most reverential, always lapsing into Sir Walter Scott, is fairly productive in that Southern writing. After *Huckleberry Finn*, nothing of comparable measure, until Griffith's *Birth of a Nation* (1915), which returns the Confederate relics, the Confederate tropes, to American literature, brings formally to a close Mark Twain's radical program in the 1880s, his humorous resolution of the Civil War.

NOTES

1. Mark Twain, *Adventures of Huckleberry Finn*, ed. Walter Blair and Victor Fischer (Berkeley: University of California Press, 1985), p. 153. Hereafter cited parenthetically in the text as HF.

2. *Works of John C. Calhoun*, 6 vols., ed. Richard Cralle (New York, 1854–7), vol. 2, p. 627.

3. Richard Beringer, Herman Hattaway, Archer Jones, and William N. Still, Jr., *Why the South Lost the War* (Athens: University of Georgia Press, 1986), p. 352.

4. *Mary Chesnut's Civil War*, ed. C. Vann Woodward (New Haven, Conn.: Yale University Press, 1981), p. 830.

5. Ibid. pp. 29, 39, 829.

6. Ibid., pp. 7, 836.

7. Joel Chandler Harris, *Uncle Remus: His Songs and His Sayings* (New York: Shocken Books: 1965), p. 163.

8. Thomas Nelson Page, *In Ole Virginia* (New York: Scribner's, 1887), p. 10.

9. Bernard Wolfe, "Uncle Remus and the Malevolent Rabbit: 'Takes a Limber-Toe Gem-mun fer ter jump Jim Crow,'" in *Critical Essays on Joel Chandler Harris*, ed. R. Bruce Bickley, Jr. (Boston: G. K. Hall, 1981), pp. 74–5.

10. Henry W, Grady, *The New South* (New York: Bonner's, 1890), pp. 320, 316, 315, 320, 318, 316, 244.

11. Jay B. Hubbell, *The South in American Literature, 1607–1900* (Durham, N.C.: Duke University Press, 1954), pp. 832–3.

12. Mark Twain, "A Private History of the Campaign That Failed," in *Selected Shorter Writings*, ed. Walter Blair (Boston: Riverside Editions, 1961), p. 206. Henceforth cited parenthetically in the text as PH.

13. *Mark Twain Speaking*, ed. Paul Fatout (Iowa City: University of Iowa Press, 1976), p. 106. Henceforth cited parenthetically in the text as MTS.

14. Justin Kaplan, *Mr. Clemens and Mark Twain* (New York: Simon & Schuster, 1966), p. 274.

15. Richard E. Peck, "The Campaign That ... Succeeded," *American Literary Realism, 1870–1910* 21.3 (Spring 1989): 10. See also Thomas Quirk, "Life Imitating Art: *Huckleberry Finn* and Twain's Autobiographical Writings," in *One Hundred Years of Huckleberry Finn: The Boy, His Book, and American Culture*, ed. Robert Sattelmeyer and J. Donald Crowley (Columbia: University of Missouri Press, 1985).

16. Mark Twain, *Life on the Mississippi* (New York: Hill & Wang, 1968), p. 243. Henceforth cited parenthetically in the text as LM.

17. Mark Twain, "A True Story, Repeated Word for Word as I Heard It," in *Selected Shorter Writings*, ed. Blair; p. 59. Henceforth cited parenthetically in the text as TS.

18. Grady, The New South, p. 146.

19. Ibid., pp. 148-9.

20. Forrest G. Robinson, In Bad Faith: The Dynamics of Deception in Mark Twain's America (Cambridge, Mass.: Harvard University Press, 1986), pp. 240, 139.

21. James M. Cox, Mark Twain: The Fate of Humor (Princeton, N.J.: Princeton University Press, 1966), p. 197.

HENRY B. WONHAM

Joyous Heresy: Travelling with the Innocent Abroad

Americans expended considerable energy attempting to answer criticism from European travellers in the New World during the late eighteenth and early nineteenth centuries. In their defense, writers such as Royall Tyler were understandably prone to grasp at whatever advantage they could claim, with the result that many of the earliest responses to European criticism probably provoked more amusement than respect on the other side of the Atlantic. As one of the first and best known patriots to brandish a pen in the nation's defense, Tyler helped to initiate a tradition of American response to European censure by producing his own observations of travel in England, published anonymously in 1808 as *The Yankey in London*. In a typical passage, the American writer condemns what he considers the pernicious habit among members of the most polite British society of polluting their language with "evanescent vulgarisms of fashionable colloquy," or slang. He goes on to object that "there are a number of words now familiar, not merely in transient converse, but even in English fine writing, which are of vulgar origin and illegitimate descent, which ... degrade their finest modern compositions by a grotesque air of pert vivacity."

The Yankee is especially rankled by the word "clever," which the British frequently employ to mean "skillful" or "adroit." He observes that

From *Mark Twain and the Art of the Tall Tale* (NY: Oxford University Press, 1993): 70–88. Reprinted by permission of Oxford University Press.

> Englishmen, from the peer to the peasant, cannot converse ten minutes without introducing this pert adjunct. The English do not, however, use it in the same sense we do in New England, where we apply it to personal grace, and call a trim, well-built young man, clever—which signification is sanctioned by Bailey's and the elder English dictionaries.

Had America's cultural sovereignty depended on the effectiveness of such attacks, it might have been a much longer and ultimately less successful struggle. Not surprisingly, a proposed second volume of Tyler's travel observations never appeared in print, possibly indicating that his strategy for out-Britishing the British was not terribly effective at bolstering the national pride.

Fortunately for America, more resourceful writers fashioned other weapons with which to answer the charge of cultural depravity in the New World. If the former colonists could not speak more correctly than their European critics, at least they could speak differently, in fact so differently that no degree of Old World refinement and polish could decipher the full meaning of an American's idiom. Hence when a character named Jonathan Peabody made a fictional journey to London as part of James Kirke Paulding's 1813 production of *The Bucktails; or Americans in England*, he was full of unmistakably native pride, whistling "Yankee Doodle" and bragging in defiance of his foreign critics: "I'm half horse, half alligator, and a little bit of the Ingen, I guess." Paulding's foppish British characters were thoroughly subdued by such figurative boasting, and they seemed equally befuddled by the American gift for spinning out formulations like "I guess," "I reckon," and "I calculate." Royall Tyler would have been embarrassed to hear his fictitious countryman Sam Slick brag in a similar vein of his peculiar advantage over the British in Thomas Chandler Haliburton's *The Attaché; or Sam Slick in England* (1843). Sam admits he may be inferior to his English hosts in manners and refinement, but he knows "a leetle, jist a leetle, grain more, p'r'aps," about the British "than they [know] of the Yankees." More specifically, Sam finds that "they're considerable large print are the Bull family," "you can read 'em by moonlight," whereas the narrator warns of Sam himself that "it was not always easy to decide whether his stories were facts or fictions." After "shampooing the English" in one episode, the champion of Yankee slang exclaims, "Oh dear! how John Bull swallows this soft sawder, don't he?"

Paulding, as usual, played an important role in establishing the yarn spinner's art as a national trait capable of asserting American democratic values against criticism from Europe. His *John Bull in America; or, The New Munchausen* (1825) satirized Britain's thirst for confirmation of its already firm belief that the liberated colonies were populated by wild animals and even wilder humans. The mock editor of this purportedly unfinished manuscript explains that, despite the title he has chosen, readers should be prepared to enjoy "a work of incomparable veracity." The manuscript's author, according to the editor, was an Englishman, probably a staff writer for London's *Quarterly Review*, a journal famous for its denunciations of America. While gathering observations of American life, the author disappeared without a trace, leaving only a tattered notebook behind. Finding the mysterious Englishman's work to be "of severe and inflexible truth," despite its author's occasional willingness to "stretch his belief into the regions of the marvellous," the editor has decided to publish the unclaimed manuscript. Predictably, the new Munchausen's narrative often verges on the fantastic, although in his eagerness to confirm a cultural bias, the Englishman is the last to suspect that his accounts of American brutality and vice are even partially exaggerated.

> The Governor told me a story of a man, who tied his black servant naked to a stake, in one of the neighboring canebrakes, near the city, which abound with a race of moschetoes that bite through a boot. He was left one night, in the month of December, which is a spring month in this climate, and the next morning was found stone dead, without a drop of blood in his body. I asked if this brutal tyrant was not brought to justice? The Governor shrugged his shoulders and replied, that he was now a member of Congress!

Paulding's caricature of the hopelessly credulous Englishman proved a far more convincing response to British attitudes than had Royall Tyler's haughty critique of London slang. The tall tale was readily available as a weapon that could be used against unsuspecting European travellers in America, and it was not long before American globe-trotters like J. Ross Browne, Samuel Fiske, and Mark Twain were arriving in foreign lands, armed with this slender superiority. In their dispatches to readers at home, America's travelling humorists declared their independence from traditional romantic and associationist approaches to descriptive writing about foreign cultures. Browne, for example, warned in *Yusef* (1853) that readers would find his account of experiences in Palestine more cheerful and less profound than other books on the Holy Land: "it will be seen that I have not felt it to be my duty to make a desponding pilgrimage through the Holy Land; for upon a careful perusal of the Scriptures, I can find nothing said against a cheerful frame of mind." Samuel Fiske, another popular dissenter from the "desponding" school of travel correspondence, published a memoir of his journey through Europe, North Africa, and the Holy Land in 1857 under the title *Mr. Dunn Browne's Experiences in Foreign Parts*. A typical passage tended to demystify European experience for American readers by adopting a yarn spinner's figurative and hyperbolic language:

> A German bed is a sort of coffin about five feet long and two wide, into which a body squeezes himself and passes the night completely buried in feathers, and digs himself out in the morning.... I never endured the thing but one night, during which I dreamed of undergoing no less than four distinct deaths, one by an anaconda necklace, one by a hempen ditto, one by the embrace of a grizzly bear, and a fourth by the press of a cider-mill.

Fiske's humor may have been less than overpowering, but his focus on sordid details rather than historical panoramas marked an important coming of age in the American interpretation of its past. His prefatory remarks, echoing Browne's disclaimer in *Yusef*, signaled an intention to describe foreign lands as they might have appeared to the eye of an unromantic American:

> I shall endeavor ... to keep wide open my eye financial, agricultural, commercial, architectural, legal, critical, metaphysical, and quizzical. I shall also take a bird's eye view of the feathered tribes, cast a sheep's eye at the flocks and herds, and obtain dissolving views of the beet sugar crop and salt mines.... No rouge will be laid on the face of the old lady,

and no artificial helps resorted to, to improve her beauty; no milliner's fripperies, trinkets, and jewels, but a simple dress. Mine shall be a "plain, unvarnished tale:" no quips and quiddities, sly innuendoes and oddities of language to disturb the digestion of an after dinner reader.

In June 1867, ten years after the publication of Fiske's book, Mark Twain boarded the *Quaker City* and followed an almost identical route toward the East, determined, like his predecessors, to dispense with the conventional picturesque mode and to report his experience in a language and from a perspective that Americans could understand. Like Paulding's Jonathan Peabody and Haliburton's Sam Slick before him, Mark Twain's narrator arrives in the Old World with only a yarn spinner's shrewdness to compensate for an abundance of ignorance. But that small advantage is decisive in establishing the perspective of Twain's American innocent abroad. The narrator is aware that many experiences escape his unrefined appreciation, yet he neither apologizes for his rough humor nor makes pretenses toward understanding what is alien to his sensibility. He recognizes himself as a greenhorn in matters involving European standards of taste and sophistication, yet he is always ready to strike back by exploiting the credulity of foreigners. His intention, like Fiske's, is "to suggest to the reader how *he* would be likely to see Europe and the East if he looked at them with his own eyes instead of the eyes of those who traveled in those countries before him."

Albert Bigelow Paine noted that Twain's correspondence from Europe and the Holy Land "preached heresy—the heresy of viewing revered landmarks and relics joyously, rather than lugubriously." In fact, the author's favorite strategy in the series of letters he sent to the *Daily Alta California* and to two New York newspapers between 1867 and 1868 was to view his subject matter both lugubriously and joyously, so that his humor tended to operate in the contrast between competing points of view. In a typical passage from the original series of letters, the narrator presents an exaggeratedly luxuriant image of Lake Como, explicitly mimicking the picturesque mode of landscape description: "Last night the scenery was striking and picturesque. On the other side crags and trees, and snowy houses were pictured in the glassy lake with a wonderful distinctness, and streams of light from a distant window shot far abroad over the still waters." After several more lines of indulgent scene painting, the narrator declares, "but enough of description is sufficient, I judge." Feeling he has perhaps gone too far in his praise of Lake Como, he shifts his focus to America with a digressive comment on the "wonderful translucence of Lake Tahoe," and a different sort of scene painting ensues:

> I speak of the north shore of Tahoe, where one can count the scales on a trout at a depth of a hundred and eighty feet. I have tried to get this statement off at par here, but with no success; so I have been obliged to negotiate it at fifty per cent. discount. At this rate I find some takers, perhaps you may as well receive it on the same terms—ninety feet instead of a hundred and eighty.

The narrator's juxtaposition of these two images is significant, for his sudden willingness to negotiate the claim about Tahoe's translucence punctures the romantic picture of Como as well. Moving rapidly from lugubrious description to joyous heresy, as Paine might have put it, the narrator establishes an ongoing contrast between different ways of assessing and reporting experience. Twain employs essentially the same joke in a later episode, again echoing James Hall's 1828 account of an interpretive bartering session in which competing storytellers figure truth as a relative commodity. After a lengthy account of his ascent of Mount Vesuvius, the narrator proposes an interpretive joint venture as the only hope of affording a local legend whose extravagance is too dear:

> It is said that during one of the grand eruptions of Vesuvius it discharged massy rocks weighing many tons a thousand feet into the air, its vast jets of smoke and steam ascended thirty miles toward the firmament, and clouds of its ashes were wafted abroad and fell upon the decks of ships seven hundred and fifty miles at sea! I will take the ashes at a moderate discount, if any one will take the thirty miles of smoke, but I do not feel able to take a commanding interest in the whole story by myself.

Each of America's early yarn-spinning ambassadors, from Peabody to Dunn Browne, had played some version of this game, mingling wide-eyed reverence with a native genius for subversive, irreverent talk. Fiske was particularly adept at juxtaposing panoramic descriptions with sordid particulars, a tactic already standard in more "serious" travel correspondence dating from the first part of the nineteenth century. Nevertheless, familiar as many of its comic devices must have seemed in 1869, readers greeted *The Innocents Abroad* with unprecedented enthusiasm. Other writers knew all too well how to employ the Vesuvius brand of understatement as a way of qualifying their exaggeratedly luxurious descriptions; what separated *Innocents* from its prototypes was Mark Twain's refusal to stop at the sort of contrast suggested by mere understatement—his insistence, in other words, on dramatic confrontation in favor of verbal contrast.

Twain had learned from "The Jumping Frog" and other early pieces that the narrative interest of tall humor stems primarily from the interpretive drama that surrounds the performance of a tale. Thus on his return to America in 1868, he began revising his *Alta* letters in an effort to dramatize the often static comedy of the original correspondence. It was a step that other humorists, J. Ross Browne most notably, had omitted, yet one that proved decisive as a means of organizing what Bruce Michaelson has called Twain's "pleasure tour through modes of narration." Like earlier humorous correspondents, the narrator of *The Innocents Abroad* moves rapidly and unexpectedly from one voice to another—from sentimentalism to parody, from patriotism to anti-Americanism, from silliness to sober observation. Yet in each of his guises, the narrator remains a player in the tall tale's interpretive game, and Twain's ability to give that game dramatic expression lends the book a measure of coherence that is lacking in Browne's *Yusef* and other comic travelogues of the period. Michaelson aptly describes *Innocents* as "a stylistic experiment with the principle of improvisatory play." Insofar as all improvisation is to some extent governed, the rules of that play are the rules of the tall tale's rhetorical drama, which Twain's revisions enact at every opportunity as a way of steering his "pleasure tour" toward its appointed destination.

The Vesuvius and Tahoe passages survived Twain's reworking of the *Alta* letters, yet many of the changes he undertook in preparing a manuscript for book publication reflect a conscious effort to dramatize his humorous material. The most important single change involved a shift in the narrative situation. The third in his series of fifty letters to the *Alta*, for example, begins with a description of the Moroccan port of Tangier, which the author praises with faint damnation: "This is jolly! This is altogether the infernalest place I have ever come across yet. Let those who went up through Spain make much of it—these dominions of the Emperor of Morocco suit me well enough." When he revised the passage for book publication early in 1868, Twain made only minor changes: "This is royal! Let those who went up through Spain make the best of it—these dominions of the Emperor of Morocco suit our little party well enough" (57). The substitution of "royal" for "jolly," and the omission of the slang "infernalest," may be understood simply as part of the author's stated attempt to "weed [the letters] of their ... inelegancies of expression" as a concession to eastern readers. With the more significant insertion of "our little party," on the other hand, Twain intended to prepare a dramatic context for ensuing episodes. Much like the fictive mother of the 1861 letters from Nevada, "our little party" functions throughout *The Innocents Abroad* as a portable audience, a travelling yarn-spinning community whose exchange of yarns and interpretations allows Twain to locate his narrator's verbal pranks in a situational context. The doctor, Dan, Jack, and the Youth, together with the narrator and occasional others, perform yarns, pranks, and deceptions for the entertainment of the group, and they respond as a "community of knowers" to the sanctified fictions they encounter in Europe and the Holy Land. The "I" that reports its impressions of Tangier in the *Alta* letter becomes one of "the boys" in *The Innocents Abroad*, and while the revision has little effect on the descriptive quality of the passage, its effect on subsequent episodes is significant. With Twain as its spokesman, this small community of experienced raconteurs assesses the validity of traditional European fictions with standards imported from America.

Twain was deliberate about replacing the *Alta* narrator's individual perspective with the group perspective of the book, even when such revisions contributed nothing to the humor or elegance of a passage. A sentence in the New York *Tribune* letter of November 9, 1867, for example, originally read: "The real name of this place is Cesarea Phillippi, but I call it Baldwinsville because it sounds better and I can recollect it easier." In his revision, Twain transferred the joke a few miles to the east, attributing the wisecrack to "our little party" instead of to himself: "We rested and lunched, and came on to this place, Ain

Mellahah (the boys call it Baldwinsville)" (347). The author's justification for inserting "the boys" here and in similarly curious revisions throughout the book emerges only in the longer episodes, where "our little party" comes to life and significantly alters the direction of Mark Twain's humor. In the *Alta* letter of September 22, 1867, for example, the narrator offers the following description:

> Speaking of barbers reminds me that in Europe they do not have any barber-shops. The barbers come to your room and skin you. (I use that term because it is more correctly descriptive than shave.) They have a few trifling barber-shops in Paris, but the heaviest establishment of the kind only boasted three barbers. There, as everywhere else in Europe, as far as our experience goes, they put a bowl under your chin and slop your face with water, and then rub it with a cake of soap (except at Gibraltar, where they spit on the soap and use no bowl, because it is handier;) then they begin to shave, and you begin to swear; if you have got a good head of profanity on, you see the infliction through; but if you run out of blasphemy, there is nothing for it but to shut down on the operation until you recuperate.

This is Mr. Twain of the *Alta* letters at his best, skillfully employing understatement and metaphor in a good-natured attack on the quality of European services. The narrator of *The Innocents Abroad* describes two shaving episodes, both of which focus more intensely on an actual event. The second episode, which takes place in Venice, is particularly worthy of comparison with the *Alta* version:

> The boys sent for a barber.... I said, "Not any for me, if you please."
> I wrote on. The barber began on the doctor. I heard him say:
> "Dan, this is the easiest shave I have had since we left the ship."
> He said again, presently:
> "Why, Dan, a man could go to sleep with this man shaving him."
> Dan took the chair. Then he said:

"Why, this is Titian. This is one of the old masters."

I wrote on. Directly Dan said:

"Doctor, it is perfect luxury. The ship's barber isn't anything to him."

My rough beard was distressing me beyond measure. The barber was rolling up his apparatus. The temptation was too strong. I said:

"Hold on, please. Shave me also."

I sat down in the chair and closed my eyes. The barber soaped my face and then took his razor and gave me a rake that well-nigh threw me into convulsions. I jumped out of the chair: Dan and the doctor were both wiping blood off their faces and laughing.

I said it was a mean, disgraceful fraud. (173)

Whereas the humor of the *Alta* letter is generated by Mr. Twain's versatility as a descriptive narrator, capable of working up "a good head of profanity," the book relies for its effect on a game of credulity involving several characters. In *The Innocents Abroad*, the shaving experience has become less a subject for comic description than the pretense for narrating a brief encounter between gullible and conspiring members of "our little party." As in an earlier story, which pitted the experienced Simon Wheeler against a naive and indignant Mark Twain, it is the relationship between antagonists that generates the humor of the episode.

The difference between the comic method of the letters and that of the book is even more pronounced in the scenes that describe the harassment of Italian guides. In the sixth Alta letter, dated July 16, 1867, Twain relates his experience with a Genoan guide who claims to be one of only three citizens of that city who can speak and understand English. The guide leads his patron to the birthplace of Christopher Columbus, where Twain spends fifteen minutes "in silent awe before this inspiring shrine." Only later does the guide mention that it was not exactly Columbus but Columbus's grandmother who was born there. The purported linguist then conducts the narrator to the municipal palace, where three of the explorer's letters are displayed. When asked if Columbus wrote them himself, the guide answers, "Oh, no." The narrator becomes frustrated:

I began to suspect that this fellow's English was shaky, and I thought I would test the matter. He showed us a fine bust of Columbus on a pedestal, and I said, "Is this the first time this person, this Columbus, was ever on a bust?" and he innocently answered, "Oh, no." I began to think, then, that when he didn't understand a question, he just answered, "Oh, no," at a risk and took the chances. So I said, "This Columbus you talk so much about—is he dead?" And the villain said quietly, "Oh, no!" I tested him further. I said, "This palace of the Dorias which you say is so old—is it fifty years old?" "Oh, no." "Is it five hundred?" "Oh, no." "It's a thousand, though, ain't it?" "Oh, yes." So his plan was to answer, "Oh, no," twice, always, and then, "Oh, yes," by way of a change. All the information we got out of that guide we shall be able to carry along with us, I think.

The guide's method of concealing his ignorance of English wins a few laughs in this passage, yet when Twain revised the episode for *The Innocents Abroad*, he again shifted the emphasis of his humor from language to drama. As Leon T. Dickinson has remarked in his important study of the book, the humor of the revised version no longer focuses on the guide's ignorance of English, "but rather [on] his consternation in the face of the questions put to him" by the boys. The chief inquisitor is not Mark Twain but the doctor, a consummate yarn spinner and grave humorist who, like the ideal teller described in "How to Tell a Story," "does his best to conceal the fact that he even dimly suspects that there is anything funny" about his statements. The doctor's skill is indeed considerable, according to the narrator's account, for he "can keep his countenance, and look more like an inspired idiot, and throw more imbecility into the tone of his voice than any man that lives" (209–10). Thus the episode with the Genoan guide becomes something more like a tall-tale encounter than a game of words and misunderstanding when the doctor decides to entertain his friends by fooling the unsuspecting European with his deadpan sincerity. Intending to exploit the same American fascination with Columbus that had cost Mark Twain fifteen minutes of wasted awe in the *Alta* letter, the guide leads the boys on a relic hunt:

"Come wis me, genteelmen! Come! I show you ze letter-
writing by Christopher Columbo! Write it himself! Write it
wis his own hand! Come!" ...

We looked indifferent—unconcerned. The doctor
examined the document very deliberately, during a painful
pause. Then he said, without any show of interest:

"Ah—Ferguson—what—what did you say was the name
of the party who wrote this?"

"Christopher Columbo! Ze great Christopher Columbo!"

Another deliberate examination.

"Ah—did he write it himself or—or how?"

"He write it himself! Christopher Columbo! His own
handwriting, write by himself!"

Then the doctor laid the document down and said:

"Why, I have seen boys in America only fourteen years old
that could write better than that."

"But zis is ze great Christo—"

"I don't care who it is! It's the worst writing I ever saw.
Now you mustn't think you can impose on us because we are
strangers." (210)

The irony of the doctor's last statement lies in the fact that the
guide is actually the stranger in this encounter, and his failure to
recognize the doctor's deadpan attitude provides entertainment for the
boys, who are cultural insiders despite the fact that they are on foreign
soil. The humor of the episode results not from the guide's poor English,
as in the letter, but from the dramatic consequences of his failure to
understand the doctor's tone. As in the shaving scene, the revised version
places the original verbal comedy in a situational context that is
patterned after a tall-tale performance. The credulity of cultural
outsiders like the Genoan guide and, later, the American Pilgrims aboard
the ship becomes a rallying point for the boys throughout the book.
They repeatedly challenge outsiders with the doctor's brand of veiled
absurdity, and those "tests," as the narrator calls them, allow Twain to
dramatize the encounter between Old and New World perspectives as
he had not done in the original correspondence.

In his addition of new episodes to the book, Twain pursued the
same priority of dramatization over description, and again the tall tale

provided a rough dramatic principle. In several scenes, including one that did not appear in the letters, the narrator parodies his own credulity, which is rooted in an inherited assumption of European superiority in matters of taste and refinement. In his effort to appear sophisticated by European standards, the narrator falls victim to a shop girl's straight-faced flattery:

> It seemed a stylish thing to go to the theatre in kid gloves, and we acted upon the hint. A very handsome young lady in the store offered me a pair of blue gloves. I did not want blue, but she said they would look very pretty on a hand like mine. The remark touched me tenderly. I glanced furtively at my hand, and somehow it did seem rather a comely member. I tried a glove on my left hand and blushed a little. Manifestly the size was too small for me. But I felt gratified when she said:
>
> "Oh, it is just right!" ... "Ah! I see you are accustomed to wearing kid gloves—but some gentlemen are so awkward about putting them on."
>
> It was the last compliment I had expected. I only understand putting on the buckskin article perfectly.... She kept up her compliments, and I kept up my determination to deserve them or die.
>
> "Ah, you have had experience! [A rip down the back of the hand.] They are just right for you—your hand is very small— if they tear you need not pay for them. [A rent across the middle.] ..."
>
> I was too much flattered to make an exposure and throw the merchandise on the angel's hands. I was hot, vexed, confused, but still happy; but I hated the other boys for taking such an absorbing interest in the proceedings. (55–56)

The girl's flattery is not a tall tale, but rhetorically it works the same way. The narrator's vanity and credulity cause him to misinterpret her affected sincerity, and again the performance offers priceless entertainment for the boys. As before, they play the part of cultural insiders, although it later turns out that the inside knowledge that allows them to appreciate the ruse has been won at a cost. After Dan and the

doctor soliloquize about the importance of refinement and experience in
a gentleman, the narrator learns that the boys have already attempted to
buy kid gloves and that they, too, have suffered humiliation as a result of
their vanity. In the end, their mutual victimization draws the members of
the "little party" closer together and helps to define their peculiarly
American values against those of Europe: "We threw all the purchases
away this morning. They were coarse, unsubstantial, freckled all over
with broad yellow splotches, and could neither stand wear nor public
exhibition. We had entertained an angel unawares, but we did not take
her in. She did that for us" (57).

Actually, the boys perform a twofold function in the book.
Together with enabling the author to dramatize the verbal humor of the
letters, they implicitly supply the reader with a consistent perspective
toward that humor. In his preface to *The Innocents Abroad*, Twain declares
that his reflections of travel intend "to suggest to the reader how *he*
would be likely to see Europe and the East if he looked at them with his
own eyes" (15). James M. Cox has pointed out that Twain's comment
expresses the veiled assumption that "as long as the narrator is honest,
there is no real distinction between the narrator and the reader. The
narrator's feelings and vision stand for the reader's own." In fact,
however, the narrator's gullibility and romanticism frequently inject
ironic distance between his perspective and that of the reader. Thus
when Mark Twain suddenly adopts the role of naive victim, as in the kid-
glove scene, the reader shares a laugh with the boys at his expense. "Our
little party" functions throughout the book as an ideal inside audience,
capable of inviting and sustaining the reader's sympathy whether Twain's
narrator is playing the role of spokesman or victim in the group's
entertainment.

Elaborating on this question of the narrator's flexible role, Forrest
G. Robinson voices a traditional concern about the book when he writes
of Twain's narrator that "sudden shifts of tone betray a marked
ambivalence about America, and a conspicuous incapacity to sustain a
tone of humorous impersonation." Robinson is right to observe a
conspicuous lack of stability in the narrator's tone, for *The Innocents
Abroad* is indeed a "pleasure tour through modes of narration," and
Twain seems just as comfortable playing the innocent as the old timer.
Yet the tall tale effectively structures this conspicuous instability by
establishing, instead of a consistent narrative tone, a stable rhetorical

game in which the narrator consistently participates. Whether the mode of narration is innocent or experienced, sentimental or parodic, the game unfolds among its players in essentially the same way.

The narrator's "marked ambivalence about America" also operates within the larger consistency of the tall tale's rhetorical encounter. Robert Regan has written that it was only toward the end of the journey, in September 1867, that Twain finally discovered "the theme that was to constitute the bedrock of *The Innocents Abroad*." In his thirty-seventh letter to the *Alta*, according to Regan, in which the correspondent describes the hypocritical piety of the *Quaker City's* pilgrims, "Mark Twain for the first time winnows chaff from wheat, separates 'pilgrims' from 'sinners,'" and thus settles on "the theme of his first great work." "Without foreshadowing," Regan continues, "a dramatic antagonism made its appearance." Whereas guides were easy prey because they failed to understand "our little party's" sense of humor, the *Quaker City's* American pilgrims came to represent a more formidable opposition to the attitudes expressed by the narrator and his friends. The pilgrims not only fail to appreciate the narrator's humor; they reject it with a self-righteousness that he never observes in even the most repellent foreigners. Their narrow and inflexible vision of truth leads them on more than one occasion to "commit a sin against the spirit of religious law in order that they might preserve the letter of it." Citing scriptural authority, the pious tourists cruelly misuse their horses rather than risk breaking the Sabbath, and later they desecrate sacred shrines in order to collect reminders of their journey through the Holy Land (323). Zealously determined to parade their piety before the world, they embody the hypocrisy of what Twain elsewhere deemed "the most malignant form of Presbyterianism,—that sort which considers the saving of one's own paltry soul the first and supreme end and object of life."

As he revised the *Alta* correspondence for publication, Twain sought to project his new theme by juxtaposing the interpretive assumptions of the pilgrims against those of "our little party," a plan that required some important changes. In the original letters, for example, a character named Mr. Blucher had served as the vernacular foil for Mr. Twain's romantic and picturesque idiom. Blucher appears frequently in the *Alta* correspondence, where he characteristically interrupts the narrator's ornate descriptions with a contradictory horse-sense comment or a deflating observation, much as the crude Mr. Brown repeatedly interrupts the romantic Mr. Twain in the author's Hawaiian letters. Yet as the revision began to take shape, Twain recognized the possibility of incorporating a larger theme by dissolving the Twain–Blucher character axis, and as a result Mr. Blucher is almost entirely absent from the text of *The Innocents Abroad*. Blucher's irreverence and the narrator's original romanticism converge in the perpetually shifting attitudes of the boys, who encounter a new kind of foil in the sanctimonious pilgrims. While "our little party" engages in hard interpretive bargaining over the plausibility of every secondhand report of experience, the *Quaker City*'s pilgrims cannot make sense of the narrator's willingness to negotiate over belief, for they deny the existence of any gray area between truth and lie. Franklin Rogers points out that the confrontation between the self-proclaimed sinners and their pious antagonists is only partially dramatized, yet the nascent conflict represents Twain's first extended treatment of what would become his greatest theme: the pragmatic and commonsense values of a vernacular community, whose natural idiom is the tall tale, confront the rigid beliefs of a society that sanctions conventional myths with the stamp of absolute truth.

The contest between rival approaches to interpretation and experience is waged with exemplary valor by both parties on the banks of the Jordan River. The pilgrims are determined that their experience of the sacred river conform strictly to the expectations they have transported all the way from America. Hence after a cold night in the bushes at the river's edge, they strip naked and wade into the freezing water, singing hymns. Mr. Blucher's cynical idiom is audible in the narrator's account of the adventure.

> But they did not sing long. The water was so fearfully cold that they were obliged to stop singing and scamper out again. Then they stood on the bank shivering, and so chagrined and so grieved that they merited honest compassion. Because another dream, another cherished hope, had failed. They had promised themselves all along that they would cross the Jordan where the Israelites crossed it when they entered Canaan.... While they did it they would picture to themselves that vast army of pilgrims marching through the cloven waters, bearing the hallowed Ark of the Covenant and

shouting hosannahs and singing songs of thanksgiving and praise. (430)

Finally, to the narrator's evident disappointment, Jack rescues the shattered hopes of the party by leading the way across the river "with that engaging recklessness of consequences which is so natural to youth" (433). The narrator observes that, henceforth, the real danger will issue less from the rushing Jordan than from the current of sanctimonious rhetoric that is likely to flow from the lips of the victorious pilgrims. They succeed in experiencing the Jordan River according to the clichéd expectations with which they came, and it is the cliché rather than the experience that they will carry home to America.

The narrator, of course, arrives in the Holy Land with similarly unrealistic expectations, although unlike the pilgrims he does not regard them as inviolable. His description of the same river combines a pilot's interest in detail and a yarn spinner's knack for hyperbole:

> When I was a boy I somehow got the impression that the River Jordan was four thousand miles long and thirty-five miles wide. It is only ninety miles long, and so crooked that a man does not know which side of it he is on half the time. In going ninety miles it does not get over more than fifty miles of ground. (433)

The narrator repeatedly laments the fact that "travel and experience mar the grandest pictures and rob us of the most cherished traditions of our boyhood," but his lament is insincere (433). He actually revels in a process of sudden displacement, whereby expectations vie with experience in an unending series of inversions. His allegiance lies neither with "the most cherished traditions of ... boyhood" nor with the reality that undermines them; rather, his interest is in a perpetual sequence of contrasts that he guarantees by exaggerating both the memory and the experience in his narration. In the book's first shaving scene in Paris, for example, the narrator elaborately describes the expectations instilled in his mind by secondhand reports about the luxury of Parisian barber shops.

> From earliest infancy it had been a cherished dream of mine to be shaved some day in a palatial barber shop in Paris. I

> wished to recline at full length in a cushioned invalid chair,
> with pictures about me and sumptuous furniture.... At the
> end of an hour I would wake up regretfully and find my face
> as smooth and as soft as an infant's. Departing, I would lift
> my hand above that barber's head and say, "Heaven bless you,
> my son!" (84)

This illusion is promptly deflated by the "reality" of a Parisian shave,
although the narrator's description of the event is no less extravagant
than the false expectations it displaces.

> I sat bolt upright, silent, sad, and solemn. One of the wig-
> making villains lathered my face for ten terrible minutes and
> finished by plastering a mass of suds into my mouth. I
> expelled the nasty stuff with a strong English expletive and
> said, "Foreigner, beware!" Then this outlaw strapped his
> razor on his boot, hovered over me ominously for six fearful
> seconds, and then swooped down upon me like the genius of
> destruction. The first rake of his razor loosened the very hide
> from my face and lifted me out of the chair. (85)

As James M. Cox has explained, "the 'reality' which deflates the
expectation is clearly not actuality, but an extravagant invention which,
poised against the clichés, displaces them." The narrator's "old dream of
bliss," like the other misconceptions he and the boys carry to Europe,
turns out to have been a fraud, and his description of a razor-wielding
"genius of destruction" thus supplies a preferable, although no less
outrageous, fiction. It is a preferable fiction because, like a yarn, the
narrator's account of his Parisian shave disparages illusion in favor of
self-conscious fantasy. Whereas the pilgrims successfully blind
themselves to experience by sanctifying false expectations, Twain's
narrator acknowledges the Parisian fraud for what it is and answers with
an aggressive invention of his own.

As the shaving episode makes clear, Twain's narrator is committed
to a series of exaggerated poses, and his unpredictable movement from
one to another generates much of the book's comedy. Forrest Robinson
describes this "spastic lurching" between states of innocence and
experience as a symptom of Twain's profound ambivalence, noting that

the narrator of *The Innocents Abroad* possesses "a consciousness irremediably at odds with itself, moving at great speeds between mental states, struggling quite in vain to find a comfortable point of vantage on a deeply unsettling experience." Robinson continues: "The failure to achieve this equipose between opposites and incompatibles registers in the book's characteristically nervous, at times even frantic rhythm, and in its gathering inclination to locate the source of its painful frustration not in experience but in consciousness itself." Robinson's psychoanalytic insight is acute, but his assumption that Twain's unstable narrator must be in search of "equipose" turns the book's humorous strategy into a symptom of mental unrest. Twain was quite as capable as Robinson of finding a "comfortable point of vantage" from which to describe his unsettling experience in a Parisian barber's chair, but such a description would have been far short of humorous. In his narration of the event, he chose to exaggerate both the expectation and the experience because effective humor always moves "at great speeds between mental states," and it does so precisely in order to prevent the reader from settling upon a "comfortable point of vantage." The "painful frustration" that Robinson observes in the text may in fact issue more from the critic than from the humorist, for Twain's game of juxtaposition *requires* a "divided consciousness" and a "frantic rhythm" for its effect.

Robinson and many other readers are right to notice that Twain's incessant movement between different narrative poses compromises the book's unity and coherence. At his best, however, Twain organizes the sometimes "spastic" interplay of voices in *The Innocents Abroad* by enacting the tall tale as a dramatic and rhetorical principle. In his revision of the *Alta* letters, he invented characters and episodes that enabled him to embed the verbal juxtapositions of the letters in a series of situational contexts based on the tall tale's pattern of interpretive challenge and response. Members of the narrator's "little party" gallop through foreign lands delighting in "splendid lies" and disparaging "disgraceful frauds" as they go, bargaining over the relative truth of every report and accepting the visible world as the only reliable standard. The tall tale did not resolve the contradictions inherent to the narrator's game of exaggerated contrasts, but it gave his many poses a coherent dramatic principle, a way of connecting with one another. The narrative consciousness of *The Innocents Abroad* is indeed divided, as the book's readers have always understood, but the tall tale's interpretive game allowed Twain to enact those divisions, enabling him to convert them into a form of play.

Stuart Hutchinson

Introduction to
The Adventures of Tom Sawer &
The Adventures of Huckleberry Finn

*T*om *Sawyer* (1876) and *Pudd'nhead Wilson* (1894) excepted, Samuel Clemens' best work is written in the autobiographical first person form. As we see in *Innocents Abroad* (1869), his first encounter with the Old World, and *Roughing It* (1872), his evocation of the American West, he created in Mark Twain an authorial self who was also a performing self within the narratives. Both are journey books in which Twain takes the episodes as they come, and in which nothing conclusive is promised or achieved. Each is the sum of its mainly comical adventures, though each also has an intermittently desolating undercurrent which will rise irresistibly to the surface in such final works as 'The Mysterious Stranger' (1916). *Huckleberry Finn* (1884-5) develops their method with Huck, ostensibly the creation of Twain, now at an even further remove from Clemens. Only behind the mask of a mask could Clemens in *Huckleberry Finn* engage his profoundest sense of life's comedy and tragedy, though as in all his books it was an essentially fugitive engagement. In the first paragraph of chapter 15 Huck announces the journey's destination to be 'way up the Ohio among the free states,' but as it evolves the journey is always *away from* rather than *towards*. The villages on the riverbank never get any better, and, if in nothing else, Huck is consistent in his desire to move on and not make things worse,

From *The Adventures of Tom Sawyer & The Adventures of Huckleberry Finn*, Wordsworth Classics. (Ware 2001): pp. vii–xix. Reprinted by permission.

remaining on the run because he is also never convinced he is superior to anyone he meets. This last position is why he rarely moralises, or, if he does so, as in his opening comment, 'I never seen anybody but lied, one time or another' (ch.1), offers readers the self-recognition he already has. 'Human beings *can* be awful cruel to one another' (ch.33), his response to the tarring and feathering and riding on a rail of the king and the duke, is a similar offer. Huck like any one of us might find himself joining a mob similar to the one in this scene. Like any one of us, he too might be a victim of a mob. Not that he or Twain or Clemens can be confident readers will recognise themselves in such pronouncements. Clemens and Twain cannot even be sure Huck's guilty reflections in chapters 16 and 31 on his support of Jim's escape will be read ironically, thus revealing Huck to be as essentially virtuous as slavery is morally perverted. Slavery, after all, found a justification in the American South because many normal human beings believed with Huck that aiding a Jim was wicked and would send them to hell. In *Huckleberry Finn* meanings which might offer resolution to the book's conflicts cannot even be *implied* with certainty, and Huck must remain fugitive because the book's adventures never entail, let alone reach, a clarifying destination. For related reasons he also remains inconsistent as a character, telling some jokes but not getting others, being an innocent boy but a shrewd and cynical liar, committed and oblivious to Jim. *Huckleberry Finn* offers no system of meaning in which Huck might be consistent. As its prefatory 'Notice' acknowledges in a typically unsettling joke, it endorses neither 'motive,' 'moral,' nor 'plot.' When Clemens finally settled on the pseudonym Mark Twain in 1863, after trying several others, he was not only referring to the measurement of river depths for steamboats, but also to the persistent subterfuge and double-dealing he was becoming involved in as a writer in order to tell the 'truth, mainly' (ch.1).

　　Tom Sawyer nonetheless is a simpler affair than *Huckleberry Finn*. It offers Clemens' fondest recollection of the village on the banks of the Mississippi in which he had spent his formative years and to versions of which his imagination, released in Mark Twain, recurrently returned. The real Hannibal Missouri now becomes St Petersburg as it was to become all the villages in *Huckleberry Finn*, various villages in *A Connecticut Yankee at King Arthur's Court* (1889), Dawson's Landing in *Pudd'nhead Wilson*, Hadleyburg in 'The Man that Corrupted

Hadleyburg' (1899) and even Eseldorf (in sixteenth century Austria) in 'The Mysterious Stranger.' As the novel's Preface indicates, the remembrance for the most part is indulgent in *Tom Sawyer*, Twain looking back on childhood scenes long left behind for that superior adult and more sophisticated world which 'the reader' (ch.1) is also assumed to occupy. Because this reader has nothing of the heterogeneity (black, white, American South/North, European) of readers of *Huckleberry Finn*, *Tom Sawyer* is delivered in Twain's most settled authorial voice. He is as sure of his audience outside the book as Tom, a boyhood version of the author's performing self, is sure of his audience within it. At worst St. Petersburg is irksome or boring to Tom, and he can usually triumph over it, as in the famous scene when he white-washes the fence. To us, St. Petersburg is mostly amusing, notwithstanding chapters 11 and 18, when the town verges on providing material which in *Huckleberry Finn* will propel Huck into haunted flight. Even conscience, an incubus to several of Twain's fictional selves and especially to Huck, is appeasable in *Tom Sawyer*. Whereas in other works it is such a source of irresolvable guilt that the Huck of *Huck Finn* can declare, 'If I had a yaller dog that didn't know no more than a person's conscience does, I would pison him (ch.33), in *Tom Sawyer* it presses Tom to do achievable good things, such as saving Muff Potter at his trial. This reassurance is matched by presenting Huck Finn himself as no more than a picturesque rebel, though he finally sows seeds from which his subsequent adventures will grow. If there is a spark of the later work's irony in Huck's comments about eating with the 'mighty good nigger,' Uncle Jake (ch.29), it is not allowed to kindle into troublesome flame, and slavery, so fundamentally disturbing to Twain's later attempt at fond recollection in *Pudd'nhead Wilson*, hardly casts a shadow. As for the natural world, it is accommodated in *clichés* such as 'great Nature's meditation' and 'the marvel of Nature' (ch.14), though Henry Nash Smith is right to praise the Jackson's Island scenes, and to observe that the passage describing Tom's journey back to St. Petersburg, 'sounds like Hemingway' (Smith, pp. 85-6). It anticipates Huck's account of his escape from Pap in *Huckleberry Finn*, the particular writing Hemingway himself might have been referring to when he asserted that 'All American literature comes from one book by Mark Twain called *Huckleberry Finn*' (Hemingway, pp. 22-3). Also remarkable and entertaining in *Tom Sawyer* are the intimacy and directness with which

the manners and culture of a small provincial town are realised, together
with the experience of being a boy there. Twain expects us to identify
with Tom, and even though he mocks his infatuation with Becky, he
invites us to see it as typical of the pre-sexual male. Arguably, *Tom Sawyer*
enacts male pre-adolescent wish-fulfilment, culminating in the strong
male rescuing the weak and grateful female from the cave.

If Tom and Becky were to marry, they would presumably define
each other in conventional gender roles, and *Tom Sawyer's* conclusion
seems to offer Tom as a notable exception to several of nineteenth
century American literature's other figures, including Huck. In contrast
to their endless commitment to autonomy, whatever the torments of
loneliness and estrangement, Tom is finally left with great wealth, a good
chance of marrying the community's top girl, and the prospect of an
influential place in the world. Fifty years before Fitzgerald, Twain
seemingly writes of a Gatsby legitimised and likely to get his girl. Since
Tom will never grow up, however, his future remains a proposition, and
Tom matches Gatsby, who is himself killed before reaching fulfilment. In
Tom Sawyer too the rewards and accommodations beckoning the hero
will never be attained, and dispossession prevails at least by implication.
It supports what Cynthia Griffin Wolff sees as Tom's 'final identification'
(Wolff, p. 104) with Injun Joe, the novel's most alienated figure. Each
character enabling the creation of the other, Tom can be the acceptable
rebel because the violence with which Twain's imagination scourged the
world in other books is villainised in Injun Joe. While Tom would be a
Sir Galahad to a womankind whom the author himself can denigrate as
"sappy women" (ch. 34), Injun Joe has other desires: 'When you want to
get revenge on a woman you don't kill her—bosh! you go for her looks.
You slit her nostrils—you notch her ears like a sow's!' (ch.30). Yet the
first cause of the antagonism between Injun Joe and St. Petersburg is
never established, and it is not apparent who was originally in the wrong
in the grudge he bears against Dr. Robinson. Nor is it is clear on what
charge, apart from vagrancy, the Widow Douglas's husband had Injun
Joe jailed and 'horsewhipped' (ch.30). Presumably, Twain does not want
a rational cause and effect explanation for him. As the offspring of
passions probably rapacious on the white side, Injun Joe's function is to
be bogeyman and scapegoat. Like other mysterious strangers arriving in
communities in Twain's fiction (notably in 'The Man that Corrupted
Hadleyburg' and in 'The Mysterious Stranger' itself), he undermines

whatever security the author and townspeople have, whether it be religious belief, or assumptions about their own virtue and courage. If, in Helen L. Harris's words, he is Twain's demonstration to whites of 'the typical Indian's treachery, murderousness, cowardice and depravity' (Harris, p. 499), he is also to Tom and his author what Orlick is to Pip and Dickens in *Great Expectations*, namely the estranged self destined to a desolate fate. Among Tom's fantasies of escape, the desire to 'join the Indians' (ch.8) provides the only scenario native to America. 'Injun Joe infested all [Tom's] dreams' (ch.25), because he is the nightmare of these fantasies of self-gratifying adventure. No wonder Tom feels 'an abounding sense of relief and security,' as he stands over of his dead body. With the death of this 'bloody-minded outcast' (ch.34) nightmare can be thought to be at an end.

In Leslie Fiedler's words, however, *Tom Sawyer* and *Huckleberry Finn* are 'the same dream dreamed twice over, the second time as nightmare; though to be sure, the terror of the second dream is already at work in the first, whose euphoria persists strangely in the second' (Fiedler, p. 568). Death itself means nightmare is never at an end in Twain's work, and it is in Injun Joe's death that he and Tom have their deepest identification with him. Representing the possible desolation of death for us all, it demonstrates human insignificance amid time's ceaseless immensity. Inevitably, there is rhetorical extravagance at this juncture, because heavy themes are injected into a novel too light to carry them. *Huckleberry Finn*'s superiority is that it can always bear its author's profoundest concerns, as we see immediately in the last two paragraphs of chapter 1 when Huck feels 'so lonesome I most wished I was dead.' To get Shakespeare off its back *Huckleberry Finn* will comically demolish Hamlet's 'To be, or not to be' soliloquy, 'the most celebrated thing in Shakespeare' (ch.21), but this literal deconstruction follows the creation of an American equivalent in these initial paragraphs. Like *Hamlet*, *Huckleberry Finn* will respond variously to death, the morbid Emmeline Grangerford's drawings and poems, and the sublime king's wonderfully funny claim that the dead Peter Wilks in his coffin, 'lays yonder, cold but joyful' (ch.25) being but two of the responses. In these paragraphs Huck like Hamlet is both tempted and oppressed by death, and neither the physical nor metaphysical world offers consolation. The stars shine. The leaves rustle. The wind whispers. A restless ghost grieves in the woods. Obviously, this is not the sensibility of an innocent young boy. Huck has a number of functions for his creator, and to be boy reporter of experience, unconscious of its implications, is only one of them. He is best seen as allowing unresolved versions of the authorial self (especially younger and older) to engage with its formative American world. He is never given a substantial dramatic life, precisely because these versions remain unreconciled and cannot, therefore, be offered in a consistent character having a developing cause and effect relationship with events. He remains a voice, and if he always sounds the same, as certainly his vernacular prose always looks the same, tensions and contradictions live irrepressibly within this apparent sameness. Take Huck's observation at the Widow Douglas's that, 'By-and-by they fetched the niggers in and had prayers, and then everybody went off to bed' (ch.1). From Twain's older perspective it is easy to read this as irony, his and readers' conscience about slavery being pricked by Huck's unconscious acceptance of it. Huck's response (presumably that of the author as a boy) has, nonetheless, an equal life in the book, Twain recognising that he has been capable of both his young and older views about slavery and, as representative human being, may still be capable of either or their equivalents. No state of being in *Huckleberry Finn* has precedence. Huck is a typical nineteenth century American literary voice (and thus unlike the narrator of *Great Expectations*) in that he will not grow into a final moral understanding which the author is also offering the reader. *Huckleberry Finn* is written in the past tense, but unlike *Great Expectations* we have no sense of the present to which its past has led. Precedence is aborted, because there is no developing sense of time, and no end from which author, narrator or readers can get a fix on any moment of the narrator's past life. In common with other works of nineteenth century American literature such as *Moby-Dick* and 'Song of Myself,' the only end *Huckleberry Finn* recognises is death. Except for Miss Watson's freeing of Jim, which is extraneous to the adventures, there is no end on the way to *the* end, such as is offered by the integral plots and developing moral and time schemes of contemporaneous English novels.

The sentence about the niggers and prayers reveals the author's experience of complicity in slavery. The sensibility enacted in *Huckleberry Finn* can reach to tragedy, because like Hamlet's it knows it is inevitably stained by the sullied world from which it can wish to be free. As when Huck accidentally flicks a spider to its death in a lighted candle (ch.1), it is as if we cannot inhabit the world without participating in violations. Twain's wonderful, seemingly effortless prose then records the town clock striking midnight with an ominous 'boom,' while 'twelve licks,' announcing another insistent circling day, suggests the punitiveness of time. What is it but adventures and relationships that relieve this relentlessness? What else postpones consciousness of the end? 'That was good!,' says Huck, as he hears Tom Sawyer's signal. As for, 'there was Tom Sawyer waiting for me' (ch.1), who can doubt the relief and gratification these words express? Readers of *Huckleberry Finn* may feel they must respond to Tom with derision, and Twain himself was so ambivalent towards this centre-stage artist, that even in *Tom Sawyer* he is momentarily struck by 'all the vicious vanity that was in him' (ch.19). Huck, however, remains full of admiration for his friend. In a world where to leave one village on the riverbank is to run into equal problems in another, Tom's games try desperately to enact what games are supposed to provide. They offer pleasure which is forgetfulness of trouble. 'Being Tom Sawyer was easy and comfortable' (ch.32), because in this identity humankind forgets its cares, including people needing immediate material aide. This dilemma is what the human condition involves us in, and like us all Tom is victim of, and contributor to, this condition. While Huck's final separation from him is a necessary criticism of his wilful indulgence in distraction, we can have no confidence that escape into the 'Territory ahead of the rest' (ch.43) will be more fulfilling than the escapades Tom has scripted. We might see the problematic final chapters of *Huckleberry Finn* as sharing the insights of Poe's 'The Fall of the House of Usher' and James's *The Portrait of a Lady*. In all three works the New World imagination presents the enervation of Old World structures, while having a dependency on them. It is as if there might, after all, be nothing beyond Tom's European books, or the European domains of Roderick Usher and Gilbert Osmond. Old World structures, when all is said, have enabled people to live with the endlessness of injustice, with the difference between what we want and what we can get, with the fact that after Jim is free there will always be someone else in equal trouble. That Jim should need to be freed in America demonstrated the New World as not all that new. Like the Old World, it too depended for justice on the very energies that had corrupted it.

The final adventures at the Phelps' are longer than their worth, but why should we expect them to have anything to do with the realistic freedom-quest of an adult male slave who is also a husband and a father? This version of Jim, never more than intermittent, would not have got involved with the *Walter Scott* in chapters 12 and 13, so soon after fleeing his owner. Above all, he would never have continued past Cairo to where he knows 'he'd be in the slave country again and no more show for freedom' (ch.16). The history of the composition of *Huckleberry Finn* bears crucially on this issue. As Victor A. Doyno has shown, Twain began writing the book in the summer of 1876, reaching at this time the current chapters 15-17 when the realistic plot involving Jim, and announced in the first paragraph of chapter 15, would need to be developed. At this decisive juncture he abandoned the book, not returning to it till 1879 and then ignoring the plot entirely. Later it was further undermined by the insertion of the Walter Scott material into chapters 12 and 13, though this material was actually written in 1883 along with the escapades at the Phelps'. As we now have it, therefore, when the intention to 'go way up the Ohio amongst the free States' (ch.15) duly comes along, it merely signals the possibility of one kind of *Huckleberry Finn* even as the book is already becoming another. This latter *Huckleberry Finn* is inclusive of the realistic plot but not determined by it, because there is no authorial conviction that life in an overall sense can ever improve. Consequently, the raft drifts in the current of a river mightier than human designs towards an ocean still mightier, a natural end (like death itself) in relation to which all other ends may be as contrived as Tom's games.

Even from the beginning there is a manifest degree of contrivance in the way the book's material is displayed. When Huck is kidnapped by pap, for example, it is unbelievable that he never 'got a chance to run off' (ch.6). He and pap cannot be together every minute of the day, and the mighty river of opportunity always beckons the resourceful Huck. The novel, however, needs to arrange an extended engagement with pap, because the question of how to stay free and on the run from civilisation without becoming a pap is central to its themes. Because Huck shares pap's powerful distaste for society's restraints and shaping forces, and because pap is his only known parent, answers cannot be other than complicated and incomplete. In the very funny account of pap's adventures with the new judge (ch.5) the balance of the narrator's and the author's support undoubtedly comes down on pap's side, as he abets Twain's habitual pillorying of sentimental gentility. Similarly, the prejudice and paranoia in pap's tale of his encounter with 'a free nigger' (ch.6) are realised by Twain with a fascination and comic effect beyond easy condemnation, even as pap unwittingly subverts his own position by his own utterance. Pap can be intriguingly self-conscious, as when he becomes a profane version of 'Ollie' from *Laurel and Hardy*, kicking a tub with his toes exposed, indulging in an aria of 'cussing' (ch.6) and then commenting on his cussing skills. His alcoholic frenzies are partially self-induced even to the point of fearful hallucination, suggesting his most compelling life is with his demons, as when he sees Huck as 'the angel of Death' (ch.6). A father can be as guilty about a son as a son about a father, and which son fleeing a father can be can be sure he is not fleeing himself? Huck's elaborate faking of his death, when he escapes from pap, indicates the extremity of his desire to be rid of his identity as pap's son, but it also re-enacts the insecurity and self-despair confessed earlier ('I most wished I was dead'), and not entirely provoked by pap. Perhaps a son is most secure in remembering even such a father with the resignation Huck manifests later, when he participates in Twain's comic accommodation of the character. If not, the murderousnous of Colonel Sherburn's killing of Boggs, another version of the unruly pap, may result. Even the new judge finally has violence in mind with regard to pap. Having discovered the impotence of social and legal restraints, 'he said he reckoned a body could reform the ole man with a shot-gun, maybe, but he didn't know no other way' (ch.5). Here, only the joke separates Huck and Twain from Sherburn's kind of violence. Huck, nonetheless, must remain inextricably involved with pap, as Jim recognises when he witholds from Huck knowledge of pap's death until necessity compels revelation.

Huck's amused remembrance of pap is evident at the beginning of the description of Colonel Grangerford (ch.18). In this figure the elemental forces realised in the major characters in *Huckleberry Finn* are again apparent in 'the blackest kind of eyes, sunk so deep back that they seemed like they was looking out of caverns at you,' and in the 'lightening' that can 'flicker out' from these eyes. What keeps these fearsome energies under control is an exacting performance as a gentleman in the daily costume of 'a clean shirt and full suit from head to foot made out of linen so white it hurt your eyes to look at it.' Whatever is in the caverns behind the colonel's eyes finds ultimate release in a fight to the death with a family exactly like his own, a form of self-hatred. No-one can remember the first cause of this feud, but even in this respect it is offered as inherent human conflict rather than one we can mockingly feel superior to. It is not as if the participants were uniquely stupid in listening to sermons about brotherly love and then killing one another. Because no amount of religion, wisdom, and love has ever eradicated such killing from our dealings with one another, Huck himself cannot escape a representative complicity in it: 'I reckoned I was to blame, somehow' (ch.18). The dead Buck could as well be a dead Huck, just as any of the corpses littering our screens in life's perpetual conflicts could as well be any of us. If only plots as dubious as the conflicts themselves may save us from such a fate, what may save us from the desperation of those at the camp-meeting (ch.20)? Here, in the novel's general population, we meet again the complexity of energies embodied in pap and Colonel Grangerford. Eventually we move into a 'shed,' where one of the preachers is reaching the climax of his performance, and we see people so moved by a vision of 'Glory' that they become 'just crazy and wild.' Heights and depths, if they can be distinguished, are sought by the same appetites and passions, as people with the eternal physical and spiritual maladies look for succour and are often, as by the king, taken for a ride. Even our best qualities, such as hospitality, may betray us. The king 'was invited to stay a week; and everybody wanted him to live in their houses, and said they'd think it was an honour.' These adventures and the subsequent episode when Sherburn kills Boggs (ch.21) express the living plenitude of Twain's imagination. Entering Sherburn's town with Twain's movie-camera, we encounter the 'loafers' and become aware that Twain can give a reality to loafing unacknowledged by the idealising Whitman in the opening lines of 'Song of Myself.' Hogs rest in the deep mud of the streets and, as the riverbank caves in, houses slide into the water. In this barely choate location Sherburn wants to keep up standards, while Boggs, himself desperate in such a place, periodically gets drunk and cuts loose. They are opposites entailing each other, the colonel being a Twain/Huck trying to settle for civilisation, while Boggs recalls the disparaging pap. Sherburn commands the narrative at this stage, because its voice momentarily identifies with him, even as perspectives other than his are also maintained. Some people, for example, are more relaxed about Boggs' rampaging than the apparently humourless Sherburn can ever be. They try to save Boggs by sending for his daughter, revealing themselves not to be as entirely Yahoo-like as Sherburn claims, though they are 'pretty soon ... squirming and scrounging and pushing' to look at the dead Boggs lying in a store-window with a Bible on his breast. Huck looks too, for who could resist it? Who would not want to watch the shooting re-played, if only to evaluate the actor's performance? One might not join the lynching mob, visualised by Twain (ch.22) as if he were the elder Breughel, but Huck is there if only to see what happens. He hears Sherburn voicing Twain's own contempt for mobs, though the colonel's leaves him in a lonely dead-end, even despising an army as a mob. Which cause would he share with his fellows, and what is he left with apart from violent expressions of personal will?

What do all these adventures leave Clemens and Twain with? At best their implied consciousness is some moves ahead of Huck. 'It's lovely to live on a raft' (ch.19), white and black in harmony with each other and nature, but nature cannot be relied on for succour, as is evident when the snake bites Jim (ch.10), during the fog (ch.15), and in the thunderstorm (ch.9), when nature itself is as full of contradiction as is humankind, its energy evoking the terms 'lovely,' 'wild,' 'glory,' and 'sin.' Whatever your refuge, history's disharmonies descend, returning the identities of white boy and black slave you hoped you had shed. They are returned again by king and the duke, the former recalling pap, who like the ghost in *Hamlet* persistently haunts his son. The adventures get Jim nowhere. Never in control of his fate, he is freed because 'Old Miss Watson died two months ago, and she was ashamed she was ever going to sell him down the river, and *said* so; and she set him free in her will' (ch.42). In the sense of developing to an end different from its beginning the raft-journey has never been a journey. Topographically, therefore, its distinct stages on the river have not been marked out (the first paragraph to chapter 31 is exceptional), all the villages being different versions of the same village. Whenever Huck himself in crucial reflections about his involvement with Jim shows signs of developing towards an enlightened moral consciousness about slavery (the kind of development in the narrator which *must* be replicated in a developing narrative), Twain, who is not writing a developing narrative, aborts this possibility. On the first occasion he abandoned the book for three years only to resume it at the Grangerford's with the possibility ignored. On its reprise, when Huck decides 'All right then, I'll *go* to hell' (ch.31), the author forsakes the turning point by moving the book into the escapades at the Phelps'. He has indeed an investment in not allowing Huck to develop the moral sense, which might decide slavery is wrong, and which might be associated with a journey towards an end. In a notebook entry of August 1895 he described *Huckleberry Finn* as 'a book of mine where a sound heart and a deformed conscience come into collision and conscience suffers defeat.' Adapting these terms we can see that during his crucial reflections on Jim, Huck is 'sound-heart' and 'deformed-conscience' in that his heart cannot be other than sound, nor his conscience other than deformed. He does right, but cannot think right, and is thus the reverse of what is normally human. Our moral sense may allow us to think right, but it cannot guarantee we do right, and Twain's later works, especially 'The Mysterious Stranger,' reveal how enraged he was by the frequent impotence, or self-contradictory results, of moral sense. One of the Hucks in *Huckleberry Finn*, therefore, will by-pass these complications. Endowed with the incorruptible and intuitive goodness of a sound-heart this Huck, in crises over Jim, will do good despite deformed-conscience. This Huck, moreover, must journey nowhere, because he is never allowed to develop so as to recognise the possibilities of his own virtue. Not that this is a position Twain can rest on. As in all great books, the authorial imagination in *Huckleberry Finn* turns critically on any thesis it advances. With respect to Jim and slavery, therefore, readers may think right, even though Huck cannot. Irony allows them the moral development withheld from the narrator, and in Christian terms they may become convinced that heaven, not hell, awaits Jim's rescuer. Twain is too much of a realist to believe uncritically in the absoluteness of intuition, even the intuition of the nineteenth century's Romantic child. If Huck's 'doing whichever come handiest at the time' (ch.16) could lead to a life on the raft in harmony with nature, it could equally result in pap's degradation. Worst of all, abandonment of moral sense produces Sherburn's murder of Boggs.

Even Miss Watson's remorse can be seen as a critique both of Huck's incapacity for moral sense with respect to slavery, and also of the book's fundamental disbelief in development. Miss Watson gives Jim freedom; Huck gets him nowhere. She recognises she has been wrong, and in a very minor key hers is the moral development of many of literature's heroines and heroes. Conscience such as hers is what we traditionally rely on for rectification of evil. The presupposition is that the moral sense complicit in evil can, because of conscience, transform itself and remedy evil. In Miss Watson Twain acknowledges this presupposition's contribution to human affairs, but signals his scant faith (and impending cynicism and nihilism which only the comedy restrains) by not having the adventures achieve an end. Equally, he can acknowledge a book which would have taken Huck and Jim 'among the free States' (ch.15). *Huckleberry Finn* is plural in its sense of possibility, though it sides with the Melville of 'Benito Cereno' in seeing slavery as evidence of the human condition's inherent blight. There *are* 'free States.' Slave owners like Miss Watson *can* be converted. Readers of the book, experiencing Huck's contortions of conscience, *have* been convinced of slavery's preposterousness and enormity. On the raft there *can* be absolute equality. All these possibilities hold true, yet the evil and injustice of the world remain a constant quantity, no matter which instances are remedied. In *Huckleberry Finn* Twain wants to confirm particular possibilities of arrival, while maintaining the sense of a journey without destination through moral and metaphysical conditions which never change.

For Jim the consequences are that he plays a variety of roles, one of which is the fleeing slave also depicted in a number of pre-Civil War anti-slavery narratives. This last identity is obvious, but it should be recognised that there could have been a simpler *Huckleberry Finn* without Jim. There could have been a Jim-less, open-ended book, in which adventures between Huck and Tom are the occasion for the social panorama we get for much of the time. What Jim's presence as fleeing slave demands is an end. In a book without development or destination, Jim's case requires both, and because of it the drift of Twain's fatalistic novel is brought to a self-questioning halt in chapters 16 and 31, when Huck is forced to consider what his involvement with Jim entails, and when Twain, through ironical subterfuge (even *post*-Civil War), is forced to address slavery. Even if all human plots are corrupt, Jim needs a plot which might result in his freedom whatever else it might result in. That he is given the dignity and self-respect, which are the inherent right of every human being, but which Miss Watson's remorse might not have recognised, is beyond question. The basis of the book's enduring moral case against slavery, they are expressed in what Jim will not take from Huck, in what he believes the equality of friendship entitles him to: "Dat truck dah is *trash*; en trash is what people is dat puts dirt on de head er dey fren's en makes 'em ashamed" (ch.15). Note here, it is Jim who is the moral arbiter. It is he who is ashamed of Huck. Presumably, he is never given this stature again, at least not in direct dramatisation, because it would make irresistible demands on the drift of the adventures, and this being so many of Twain's other presentations of him are questionable. We may accept that the vitality of his engagement with mystery and the metaphysical (in the marvellous inventiveness of his dream in chapter 2 and fortune-telling in chapter 4) gladden the book. Seen thus, these episodes become a comedy of wonder at human resourcefulness amid dimensions of experience of which Jim is no more a master than is anyone else. They are like the self-delight Shakespeare takes in Bottom in *A Midsummer Night's Dream*. Not so, however, when Jim is reported to be 'satisfied' at being dressed up in 'King Lear's outfit,' painted 'all over a dead solid blue,' and advertised as a '*Sick Arab—but harmless when not out of his head*' (ch.24). Here it is impossible to accede to Twain's assumption that no allegiance to a character should get in the way of a joke. Nor can we ever be untroubled by the farce at the Phelps' which requires Jim and another black man to become subservient simpletons. Great books, nonetheless, are not written from within the stockade of unblemished moral positions which critics may find it easy to occupy. In Yeats' words from 'The Circus Animals' Desertion' they begin 'In the foul rag-and-bone shop of the heart,' which for Twain meant particularly his knowledge of complicity in slavery, his inheritance of original sin. Degrees of evasiveness accompanied even the completeness of this knowledge, as they also accompanied the comedy proffering relief. Ralph Ellison authoritatively addresses these tensions in recognising that 'Jim is not simply a slave, he is a symbol of humanity,' but also in pronouncing that Jim is 'a white man's inadequate portrayal of a slave' (Ellison, pp. 32, 58).

WORKS CITED

Victor A. Doyno, *Writing 'Huck Finn': Mark Twain's Creative Process*, University of Pennsylvania Press, Philadelphia, 1991.

Ralph Ellison, *Shadow and Act*, Vintage Books, New York, 1972.

Leslie Fiedler, *Love and Death in the American Novel*, Cleveland and New York, 1962.

Ernest Hemingway, *Green Hills of Africa*, Jonathan Cape, London, 1936.

Helen L. Harris, 'Mark Twain's Responses to the Native American.' *American Literature*, 46, Jan. 1975, pp. 495–505.

Henry Nash Smith, *Mark Twain: The Development of a Writer*, Harvard University Press, Cambridge, Mass., 1962.

Cynthia Griffin Wolff, '*The Adventures of Tom Sawyer*: A Nightmare Vision of American Boyhood,' *The Massachusetts Review*, 21, Winter 1980, pp. 637–52.

Chronology

1870	Marries Olivia Langdon, February 2; edits *Buffalo Express*.
1871	Moves to Hartford with his new family; lecture tours.
1872	*Roughing It* published; lecture tour in England.
1873	*The Gilded Age* published; lecture tour in England.
1876	*The Adventures of Tom Sawyer* published.
1878–79	Lives in Europe.
1880	*A Tramp Abroad* published.
1882	*The Prince and the Pauper* published.
1883	*Life on the Mississippi* published.
1884–85	Lectures with George W. Cable; establishes publishing house, Charles L. Webster & Co.
1885	*Adventures of Huckleberry Finn* debuts.
1888	Honorary M.A. degree conferred by Yale.
1889	*A Connecticut Yankee in King Arthur's Court* published.
1891–95	Family lives in Europe due to financial troubles.
1894	Paige typesetter failure; Webster Co. in bankruptcy; *Pudd'nhead Wilson* published; world-wide lecture tour to pay off debts.
1896	Daughter Susy dies, August 18.
1897–1900	Lives in Vienna and London.
1901	Litt.D. conferred by Yale.
1902	LL.D. conferred by the University of Missouri.
1903	Family moves to Italy for Livy's health.
1904	Olivia Clemens dies June 5.
1907	Litt.D. conferred by Oxford.
1908	Moves to Stormfield, near Redding Connecticut.
1909	Daughter Jean Clemens dies December 23.
1910	Samuel Clemens—Mark Twain—dies at Stormfield, April 21; buried at Elmira, New York.

Works by Mark Twain

The Celebrated Jumping Frog of Calaveras County and Other Sketches. 1867.

The Innocents Abroad. 1869.

Roughing It. 1872.

The Innocents At Home. 1872.

The Gilded Age (with Charles Dudley Warner). 1873.

The Adventures of Tom Sawyer. 1876.

Old Times on the Mississippi. 1876.

A True Story and the Recent Carnival of Crime. 1877.

A Tramp Abroad. 1880.

The Prince and the Pauper. 1882.

Life on the Mississippi. 1883.

Adventures of Huckleberry Finn. 1885.

A Connecticut Yankee in King Arthur's Court. 1889.

The American Claimant. 1892.

Pudd'nhead Wilson's Calendar for 1894. 1893.

Tom Sawyer Abroad, Tom Sawyer, Detective, and Other Stories. 1896.

Following the Equator; A Journey Around the World. 1897.

The Man That Corrupted Hadleyburg and Other Stories and Essays. 1900.

Works about Mark Twain

Auden, W.H. "Huck and Oliver," *The Listener* 50 (October 1953): 540–1.

Bell, Millicent. "*Huckleberry Finn*: Journey Without End," *Virginia Quarterly Review* 58 (Spring 1982): 252–67.

Blair, Walter. "When Was *Huckleberry Finn* Written?" *American Literature* 30 (March 1958): 1–25.

Bloom, Harold, ed. *Mark Twain*, Modern Critical Views. Philadelphia: Chelsea House Publishers, 1986.

———, ed. *Adventures of Huckleberry Finn*, Modern Critical Interpretations. Philadelphia: Chelsea House Publishers, 1986.

———, ed. *Mark Twain*, Bloom's Major Short Story Writers. Philadelphia: Chelsea House Publishers, 1999.

———, ed. *Mark Twain*, Bloom's Major Novelists. Philadelphia: Chelsea House Publishers, 2000.

Cox, James M. *Mark Twain: The Fate of Humor.* Princeton: Princeton UP, 1966.

———. "Remarks on the Sad Initiation of Huckleberry Finn," *Sewanee Review* 62 (July–September 1954) 389–405.

DeVoto, Bernard. *Mark Twain's America.* Cambridge, MA, 1942.

———. *Mark Twain at Work.* Cambridge, MA, 1942.

Ellison, Ralph. "What America Would Be Like Without Blacks," *Time* (6 April 1970), reprinted in *Going to the Territory.* New York, 1987.

Fiedler, Leslie A. "Come Back to the Raft Ag'in, Huck Honey!" *Partisan Review* 15 (June 1948): 269–76.

Fisher, Victor. "Huck Finn Reviewed: The Reception of *Huckleberry Finn* in the United States, 1885–1897," *American Literary Realism: 1870–1910* 16 (Spring 1983): 1–57.

Fishkin, Shelley Fisher. "Mark Twain and Women," *The Cambridge Companion to Mark Twain*, Forrest G. Robinson, ed. New York: Oxford UP, 1995.

Florence, Don. "'Gazing Out Over the Ocean of Time': *The Innocents Abroad*," *Persona and Humor in Mark Twain's Early Writings*. Columbia: U Missouri Press, 1995.

Fulton, Joe B. *Mark Twain's Ethical Realism: The Aesthetics of Race, Class, and Gender*. Columbia: U Missouri Press, 1997.

Harris, Helen L. "Mark Twain's Response to the Native American," *American Literature* 46 (January 1975): 495–505.

Hill, Hamlin L. "The Composition and the Structure of *Tom Sawyer*," *American Literature* 32 (January 1961): 379–92.

Horn, Jason Gary. "Figuring Freedom as a Variety of Religious Experience? *No. 44, The Mysterious Stranger*," *Mark Twain and William James: Crafting a Free Self*. Columbia: U Missouri Press, 1996.

Howells, William Dean. *My Mark Twain: Reminiscences and Criticisms*. New York: Harper & Brothers, 1910.

Hutchinson, Stuart. "*The Adventures of Tom Sawyer* and *The Adventures of Huckleberry Finn*," *Mark Twain—Humour on the Run*. Atlanta: Editions Rodopi B.V., 1994.

Johnson, James L. "A Connecticut Yankee," *Mark Twain and the Limits of Power*. Knoxville: U Tennessee Press, 1982.

Jones, Alexander E. "Mark Twain and Sexuality," *PMLA* 71 (September 1956): 595–616.

Kazin, Alfred. "Creature of Circumstances: Mark Twain," *An American Procession* (New York: Knopf, 1984): 181–210.

Krauth, Leland. "Mark Twain: The Victorian of Southwestern Humor," *American Literature* 54 (October 1982): 368–84.

MacDonald, Dwight. "Mark Twain: An Unsentimental Journey," *The New Yorker* 36 (9 April 1960): 160–96.

Mailer, Norman. "Huck Finn, Alive at 100"' *The New York Times Book Review* 89 (9 December 1984): 1, 36–7.

Marx, Leo. "Mr. Eliot, Mr. Trilling and Huckleberry Finn," *The American Scholar* 22 (Autumn 1953): 423–40.

Morrison, Toni. *Playing in the Dark: Whiteness and the Literary Imagination.* Cambridge, MA: Harvard UP, 1992.

Ozick, Cynthia. "Mark Twain and the Jews," *Commentary* Vol. 99, no. 5 (May 1995): 56–62.

Pettit, Arthur G. "Mark Twain and the Negro," *Journal of Negro History* 56 (April 1971): 88–96.

————. "Mark Twain's Attitude Toward the Negro in the West, 1861–67," *The Western Historical Quarterly* 1 (January 1970): 51–62.

Pritchett, V.S. "Books in General," *New Statesman and Nation* 113 (2 August 1941): 113.

Schmitz, Neil. "Mark Twain's Civil War: Humor's Reconstructive Writing," *The Cambridge Companion to Mark Twain*, Forrest G. Robinson, ed. New York: Oxford UP, 1995: 74–91.

Smith, David L. "Huck, Jim, and American Racial Discourse," *Mark Twain Journal* 22 (1984): 4–12.

Smith, Henry Nash. *Mark Twain: The Development of a Writer.* Cambridge, MA: Harvard UP, 1962.

Stahl, J.D. *Mark Twain, Culture and Gender: Envisioning America Through Europe.* Athens: U Georgia Press, 1994: 66–84.

Towers, Tom H. "I Never Thought We Might Want to Come Back: Strategies of Transcendence in *Tom Sawyer*," *Modern Fiction Studies* 21 (Winter 1975): 509–20.

Tuttleton, James W. "Mark Twain: more 'tears and flapdoodle,'" *The New Criterion* Vol. 15, no. 1 (September 1996): 59–65.

Turner, Arlin. "Mark Twain and the South: An Affair of Love and Anger," *The Southern Review* 4 (April 1968): 493–519.

Wallace, John H. "Huckleberry Finn is Offensive," *Washington Post* (11 April 1982).

Washington, Booker T. "[Tributes to Mark Twain]," *North American Review* 191 (June 1910): 828–30.

Wolff, Cynthia Griffin. "The Adventures of Tom Sawyer: A Nightmare Vision of American Boyhood," *The Massachusetts Review* 21 (Winter 1980): 637–52.

Wonham, Henry B. "Joyous Heresy: Traveling with the Innocent Abroad," *Mark Twain and the Art of the Tall Tale*. New York: Oxford UP, 1993: 70–88.

WEBSITES

The Center for Mark Twain Studies, Elmira College
www.elmira.edu/MarkTwain/twainhom.htm
The Mark Twain Boyhood Home and Museum, Hannibal
www.marktwainmuseum.org/
Mark Twain: A Film Directed by Ken Burns
www.pbs.org/marktwain/
Mark Twain in His Time Homepage
etext.lib.virginia.edu/railton/index2.html
The Mark Twain House
www.marktwainhouse.org/
The Mark Twain Papers and Project
bancroft.berkeley.edu/MTP/
TwainWeb
www.yorku.ca/twainweb/

Contributors

HAROLD BLOOM is Sterling Professor of the Humanities at Yale University and Henry W. and Albert A. Berg Professor of English at the New York University Graduate School. He is the author of over 20 books, including *Shelley's Mythmaking* (1959), *The Visionary Company* (1961), *Blake's Apocalypse* (1963), *Yeats* (1970), *A Map of Misreading* (1975), *Kabbalah and Criticism* (1975), *Agon: Toward a Theory of Revisionism* (1982), *The American Religion* (1992), *The Western Canon* (1994), and *Omens of Millennium: The Gnosis of Angels, Dreams, and Resurrection* (1996). *The Anxiety of Influence* (1973) sets forth Professor Bloom's provocative theory of the literary relationships between the great writers and their predecessors. His most recent books include *Shakespeare: The Invention of the Human* (1998), a 1998 National Book Award finalist, *How to Read and Why* (2000), and *Genius: A Mosaic of One Hundred Exemplary Creative Minds* (2002). In 1999, Professor Bloom received the prestigious American Academy of Arts and Letters Gold Medal for Criticism, and in 2002 he received the Catalonia International Prize.

NORMA JEAN LUTZ is a freelance writer who lives in Tulsa, Oklahoma. Writing professionally since 1977, she is the author of more than 250 short stories and articles as well as 50-plus books—fiction and nonfiction.

TENLEY WILLIAMS has a Ph.D. in English from New York University. She lives in New York City, where she teaches literature and writing. She is the author of *Stevie Wonder* for the Chelsea House Overcoming Adversity series.

NEIL SCHMITZ is Professor of English at SUNY Buffalo, specializing in American literature. His publications include *Of Huck and Alice, Humorous Writing in American Literature* (1983), and *White Robe's Dilemma: Tribal History in American Literature* (2000).

HENRY B. WONHAM is Associate Professor of English at the University of Oregon, with fields of interest in 19th century American Literature and Modern Literature, British and American. In addition to his volume on Twain, his publications include *Criticism and the Color Line: Desegregating American Literary Studies* (1996), and *Charles W. Chesnutt: A Study of the Short Fiction, 1998*, ed.

STUART HUTCHINSON teaches in the School of English at the University of Kent at Canterbury, specializing in 19th and 20th century American literature. In addition to *Mark Twain—Humour on the Run*, his publications include *Henry James: An American as Modernist,*, (1982); *Twain: Critical Assessments*, ed. (1993), *George Eliot: Critical Assessments*, ed. (1996), and recent articles on Edith Wharton and Don DeLillo.

INDEX